I Married an Italian COOKBOOK

I Married an Italian COOKBOOK

by

Bette Scaloni

illustrated by **Rob Cobuzio**

AN ESSANDESS SPECIAL EDITION

NEW YORK • 1968

I MARRIED AN ITALIAN COOKBOOK

Copyright © 1968 by Bette Scaloni.

Published by *Essandess Special Editions,*
a division of Simon & Schuster,
Inc., 630 Fifth Avenue, New York, N. Y. 10020,
and on the same day in Canada
by Simon & Schuster of Canada, Ltd.,
Richmond Hill, Ontario.

PRINTED IN THE U. S. A.

To my dear husband Richard,
who somehow lived through it all.

ACKNOWLEDGMENTS

My sincere thanks go to these wonderful people who suffered through this with me and gave me their encouragement and help:

My mother-in-law Helen, Aunt Ida and Uncle Benny, Aunt Lucy, Aunt Violette, Mr. and Mrs. Donald Popolo, Mr. and Mrs. Anthony Silba, Mrs. Peter Silba, and Mr. and Mrs. Daniel Grassi.

Contents

Introduction

Remember Rudolph Valentino? Isn't Vittorio Gassman gorgeous? Does Marcello Mastroianni give you a shiver? Ah, Italian men! Dark, handsome, exciting, aware that they were born just to make women feel like women! Their soulful eyes and flashing white teeth, their charm and flattery can make you feel, for the moment at least, that you are the only woman in the universe. Well, beware, my dears, I married an Italian, and there is one serious defect in these perfect specimens of manhood — they all love Italian foods.

If you're planning to marry one of these dashing men and

you're not an Italian girl, watch out! You'll be knee deep in tomato sauce before the honeymoon is over!

Oh, he'll kiss your forehead and whisper in your ear that he doesn't care what he eats, but he doesn't mean it. He's not being insincere; he just can't help it. It's something as hereditary as tea is to Englishmen — only much more involved.

I wasn't prepared to cope with this "defect" and after my marriage I had to ask myself a soul-searching question: Can an American girl from a small farming town in the East find happiness cooking for an Italian from the shores of Naples and Messina? I was born and reared in a world far removed from those shores and believe me, in the kitchen our worlds were far apart indeed!

My husband was full of love and eager to please, the prince I had dreamed of. Our meeting, romantic courtship, and marriage all happened in the short space of four months. Breathtaking and beautiful, to be sure, but the moment of truth was yet to come.

Of course, I knew that he liked Italian food. During our courtship we'd have Sunday dinners with his mother and delightful evening suppers with his friends. I had the vague feeling then that I should learn something about Italian cooking, but my dear husband assured me that it wasn't necessary. Of course, in that romantic time, food was the farthest thing from our minds.

The tragic day finally arrived. It happened on the eighth Sunday morning of our enchanted marriage. From a nearby apartment the fragrance of the traditional Sunday sauce wafted into our window, and I saw a wistful, faraway look come into my husband's eyes as the wonderful aroma overwhelmed our tiny kitchen. Perhaps it had happened before, but I didn't notice until the eighth Sunday. I knew then that the die was cast. I'd better master Italian cooking.

This was the beginning of my happy and sometimes harrowing adventures through the labyrinth of Italian cooking.

As a bachelor, my husband had dined quite often at the

homes of friends and relatives. The little old Italian ladies who used to feed him were my competition. They loved to feed the young, single men, who were always "too thin." Mrs. Silba made the best sauce; Mrs. DiRado made the best lasagne; Mrs. Grassi made the best manicotti — there seemed to be no end to the list.

My husband had introduced me to all his friends and of course I had met all of those darling little old ladies. I never dreamed that I would soon be back, pad and pencil in hand, asking them how to cook Italian food. Each of these kind ladies welcomed me graciously and was delighted to help. They were flattered that I had come to them and probably thankful that my husband, whom they had known since birth, wouldn't languish forever on a diet of frankfurters and beans. As I sat there, they'd dart about their kitchens with great efficiency — dipping, spooning, stirring, chopping, assaulting meat with knives — I tried hard to keep up with their fast yet meticulous preparations. While I watched them prepare food, I furiously scribbled notes, trying to translate their dialects and broken English into recipes for the food my husband loved.

Sauce seems to hold the key to most Italian dishes, and there are as many ways to make it as there are villages in Italy. Take tomato sauce, for example. I asked questions about how to make it the "right way" until I was reeling with information. All the women I talked to had a different way of making it, and each considered herself a purist. How to put this wealth of information together was another thing.

Some of the more intelligible answers went like this: "Use only tomatoes packed in Italy. After all, they're Italian." "*No!* Use tomatoes from California, the rain is softer." "Use imported tomato paste from Italy, it's the only civilized way to make sauce." "*Never!* Use the paste from California, the soil is warmer." "*Mamma Mia!* Don't use any paste, it makes the sauce too bitter." "Squeeze the tomatoes through a sieve." "*Don't* squeeze the tomatoes through a sieve." "Take out the seeds." "Leave the seeds in" — there were many more such suggestions.

What to use was confusing enough, but how much to use

3

was really baffling. For instance, as simple but important a question as how much salt to put into the sauce brought some bewildering responses.

One woman, trying to be as instructive as possible, shrugged and said, "This-a-much." Another, with a sly little smile, said, "Zing-a-zing," as she waved an unknown quantity of salt into her bubbling sauce. Still another lady, even more enigmatic than the rest, stood with her back to me, rapped her wooden spoon on the pot, and said, "Eh."

It was up to me to decipher this fantastic code. Did "this-a-much" mean six grains of salt rubbed between the thumb and forefinger and slowly trickled into the sauce? Did "zing-a-zing" mean ½ teaspoon of salt mulled in the palm of the hand and waved into the sauce with verve? Did "eh" mean ¼ teaspoon of salt dropped on the traditional wooden spoon and then swatted backhand into the sauce? You can begin to understand my problems with the directions given by these kind people.

They also impressed upon me the importance of using the right foods. "You must use *real* sausage, made by Italians," one said as she untied the bright red string around the plump links. "*Real* Italian cheese," said another as she sprinkled freshly grated Pecorino cheese over heavenly looking eggplant. I soon realized that they weren't merely being chauvinistic; they had a point.

Only the finest foods find their way into an Italian kitchen. Food is one of the greatest pleasures in life and Italians take it quite seriously. No second best is allowed. My kitchen had to have the same fragrance as theirs, and there was only one way to do it. The Italian food store.

What an experience! I couldn't believe my eyes, ears, or nose as my husband ushered me through the door of a little Italian store in the heart of his old neighborhood. So much to see! Color everywhere! It was like walking into Italy! To my inexperienced eyes, accustomed to the neat rows of food in supermarkets, it was chaotic. Everything seemed to be going on at the same time. At closer inspection, though, things were pro-

4

ceeding in an orderly manner. Only the conversations seemed to be going nowhere, directed at no one; just the sheer pleasure of hearing one's voice seemed to matter.

When I started this great adventure I had visions of preparing food the way the old Italian women did: buying chickens from crates, wringing their necks, and eviscerating them. I had nightmares where I was elbow deep in chicken feathers and blood, and I said a little prayer of thanks when I discovered that the chickens in the Italian food store were cleaned and ready to cook. They were only available in their natural state if you asked for them that way, and I'd never become that much of a purist.

It was a tiny store and we inched carefully past a great barrel of black olives floating in brine and a crock filled with lupini that stood in the middle of the aisle. As a matter of fact, there weren't any aisles. There were shelves, of course, but these were piled with pottery, espresso pots, imported candy, and enormous spaghetti bowls. I almost stumbled over a bushel of garlic braided into long chains. The regular customers didn't have my problem with navigation; they traveled these uncharted areas without any apparent discomfort. They talked to each other around, over, and through whatever was between them. Their animated conversations never missed a beat and their waving arms seemed to know the location of every item in the store — they never knocked anything over.

There was a floor-to-ceiling pyramid of imported pasta, every size and shape in existence. "These are the best to use," my husband explained. "They're true pasta — not bleached." I couldn't believe the variety. To me pasta meant elbow macaroni, spaghetti, and noodles. I was fascinated by the red and blue boxes imported from Italy. I picked up a pound of Angelo Capello — Angel Hair. It was the thinnest spaghetti I had ever seen. It was hard to believe that anything could be so fragile without breaking.

The exciting smells began to identify themselves. Provalone, garlic, Romano, Pecorino, fish, smoked meats, olives,

5

mushrooms, anchovies. So exotic and tantalizing. A whole, new world was opening to me.

We approached the meat counter, and I was amazed to see five busy butchers in this little store. Customers yelled their requests to the butchers and continued their conversations at the same time. The men behind the counter cut, weighed, and wrapped meat, and kept a sharp eye on everything. As one of them was putting a tray of squid into the meat case, and with the thought of "what in the world do you do with them" in my mind, it was my turn to order. I timidly said, "One pound of sausage." *"What?"* thundered the butcher as he tried to catch my tiny voice through all the noise and confusion. I suppose I had expected a "pardon me" and I stepped back a bit startled, but my husband gallantly took over. With great authority, a level eye on the butcher, and a theatrical wave of his cigarette, he said, "She wants a pound of sausage." "Ah, sausage," the butcher said, sizing me up as a non-Italian. He wrapped the sausage and asked my husband if I cooked Italian food. The little man looked at my slight 100-pound frame as though I were a poor orphan in need of a good meal. "Of course," said my loyal spouse. "She's a great cook." He squeezed my hand.

We left the meat counter and I felt a little guilty. I couldn't cook "Italian" and yet my dear husband had defended me to these people. I was proud of him but I was in despair. I just couldn't let him down after he had told the best butcher in town that I knew how. And I didn't even know what to order! I looked over my shoulder and saw the wise old man watching me with that "another nice Italian boy going to starve" look on his face.

I asked my husband what Italians did with the squid that I had seen staring at me from the tray. "Oh, they just cook them in sauce," he said blithely. My stomach turned over. I had to learn how to cook squid. That was more than I had bargained for. I shuddered a little to myself.

After we made some basic purchases to help me get acquainted with an Italian store, we made our way to the checkout

6

counter. My husband asked me if I were sure that I wanted to learn to cook Italian food. "It's really not necessary, and I'll still love you," he said. His reassurances only made me want to try harder. Besides, it was going to be fun, I thought — well, funny, anyway.

As we stood at the counter there was a large straw basket filled with chestnuts next to my foot. Out of the corner of my eye I thought I saw something move. I looked at the basket and was horrified to see big, black things crawling all around the chestnuts! Now I'm as much for quaint atmosphere as the next person, but I felt that this was going a little too far. Shaking with indignation, I informed the storekeeper that his basket of chestnuts was crawling with bugs. He gave me a puzzled look, then peered over the counter into the basket. I was expecting an apology and was amazed to hear him roar with laughter. Pulling himself up and looking me straight in the eye, he said, "That's only lumache, lady. You know, *lumache.*" Lumache, I thought. I couldn't believe they had a name for bugs and chestnuts. I turned aghast to my husband, but he was smiling. He slowly put his arm around me and whispered in my ear, "Lumache, honey, that means snails in Italian." *"Snails!"* I blurted out. I looked at the basket again and to my utter embarrassment, saw the whole quivering, brown mass on the move.

I love seafood — lobsters, clams, things like that — but it seems that Italians love anything that swims. No matter how many times I've been in Italian kitchens, I'm still surprised at the variety of marine life I've seen marinating on the counter, hiding in a pot of sauce, or just plain living in the sink! Snails, squid, eels — I could see that cooking Italian food was going to involve a lot more than pouring sauce on macaroni.

My husband made a great joke of my embarrassment, and we all had a good laugh. The storekeeper and I eventually became good friends. You'll find that Italian storekeepers are only too eager to help a fledgling bride, especially if she's married to an Italian.

There's an old Italian proverb that says, "In the home

there should be one head and one heart." My husband and I decided to improve on this saying and use two heads and two hearts. I had to use my head to learn how to cook Italian food, and he certainly had to use his heart to eat it.

I cooked mushy pasta for a long time before I perfected it. The pasta should be cooked until it's still firm in the middle but not tough. *"Al dente"* is the phrase Italians use, which means "to the teeth." I made glorious looking meatballs, but they tasted like soap and kerosene and were as hard as bullets. My first try at ravioli ended with a large, yellow mass of dough that wouldn't unglue itself from my fingers.

I talked and listened to practically everybody in an Italian kitchen or store and eventually fumbled, overcooked, scorched, burned, and cried my way to success. The aromas of a decent sauce began to emerge from my tired pots and it really started to taste good, but there was still something missing, and I finally realized what it was. Confidence! I was putting the same ingredients into my pots that the little old women were putting into theirs. I even slung a towel over my shoulder, walked around with a large wooden spoon, and wore a Mother Hubbard apron as they did. The only difference was that they didn't worry about the outcome. The day I discovered this for myself, I prepared the best meal I ever made, and I was so proud when my husband finally said, "This is it!" Well, actually he yelled it, picked me up, and gave me a great big kiss. I cried like a baby. It had taken me almost a year. A whole year, but it was worth every minute.

Yes, Italian men do have one "defect," their love of Italian food, but this little fault in my husband turned out to be one of the happiest problems of my life. It enabled me to learn to cook Italian food properly.

Here are the recipes I successfully deciphered after much trial and error from about fourteen dialects, many sorrowful looks from my husband, and a few good cries. They have all been given the seal of approval by my very discriminating husband so authenticity is guaranteed, and, for your convenience, there's not a "zing-a-zing" or an "eh" in the lot. Just make sure you follow the directions carefully, take your time, and keep telling yourself that you can do it.

Oh, yes. One last word before you begin your adventure. Be sure to use a big, old-fashioned, wooden spoon. It commands respect and gives a dandy, reassuring "clunk" to any delectable food being born.

Soups

  There's nothing difficult about making soup. I enjoyed learning every one of these recipes and for once, I didn't have any problems, except for one simple misunderstanding. That was when I decided to make Zuppa Inglese and discovered just in the nick of time that it wasn't soup at all but Italian Rum Cake. I thought it was strange to have a soup recipe start off with a sponge cake, but then I *was* working with unfamiliar recipes.

  Soup is one of the great comforts of the world. You can have a little cupful, you can have a bowlful, or you can make a whole meal of soup. Italians like life to be comfortable, and since they've been making soup for centuries, it's only natural that their soups should be something special.

Make a pot of soup, get a loaf of crisp Italian bread and some freshly grated cheese, and have a meal fit for the gods.

Oh yes, another nice thing about making a meal from soup is that there's only one pot to wash.

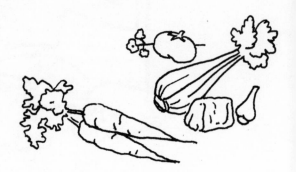

BEEF BROTH

Brodo Di Manzo

1 pound beef chuck, cut in
  1-inch pieces
1 shank bone with marrow
6 quarts cold water
Salt to taste
1 stalk celery, quartered

1 carrot, quartered
2 small onions, whole
2 tomatoes, halved
2 tablespoons parsley,
  chopped

Place meat and marrow bone in deep pot with cold water and bring to a fast boil. Reduce heat and remove foam from top of water. Add remaining ingredients, cover, and simmer slowly about 3 hours. Remove meat and use as desired. Remove marrow from bone, and strain broth, marrow, and vegetables. Store in glass container in refrigerator. May be used as broth or stock for soup.
Makes about 6 quarts.

BEEF BROTH WITH POTATO DUMPLINGS

Brodo Di Manzo Con Gnocchi

1 cup mashed potatoes
2 tablespoons olive oil
1 egg, beaten
3 tablespoons Romano
   cheese, grated

Salt to taste
Dash of nutmeg
Olive oil for frying
1 quart beef broth

Place first 6 ingredients in bowl and mix well. Sprinkle flour on pastry board, and roll out dough in long, pipelike strips, about ¾ inch thick. Sprinkle strips with flour and cut in ¾-inch pieces. Shape pieces into balls and fry in hot oil until golden brown. Drain and serve in hot beef broth.
Serves 4 to 6.

SOUP WITH BEEF

Minestrone Con Manzo

3 cups beef, cooked and diced
4 quarts water
4 small onions, whole
2 cups Italian tomatoes
1 clove garlic, halved
Salt and pepper to taste
2 stalks celery, diced

1 tablespoon parsley, chopped
2 carrots, diced
2 medium potatoes, diced
1 cup green beans, chopped
1 cup Ditalini
Romano cheese, freshly
   grated

Put beef and water in large pot and bring to boil. Lower flame and add onions, tomatoes, garlic, salt, pepper, celery, and parsley. Cover and simmer for 2 hours. Add carrots, potatoes, and green beans. Simmer for 45 minutes more. Add Ditalini and cook until tender. Serve with grated cheese sprinkled over the top.
Serves 6 to 8.

CHICKEN BROTH

Brodo Di Pollo

1 stewing chicken, 3 or 4
  pounds
4 quarts cold water
1 stalk celery, quartered,
  with leaves

1 medium onion, halved
Salt and pepper to taste
3 sprigs parsley

Put all ingredients in deep pot. Bring to a boil for 10 minutes; remove foam from top of water. Cover and simmer about 3 hours or until meat is ready to fall off bones. Remove chicken and use as desired. Strain vegetables and broth. Store in glass container in refrigerator. Use as stock or broth.
Makes about 4 quarts.

ASPARAGUS SOUP WITH CHICKEN

Zuppa Di Asparagi Con Pollo

1 pound asparagus, cleaned
  and cut in 3-inch pieces
½ clove garlic
2 quarts chicken broth
1 chicken breast, cooked and
  chopped
½ cup rice, uncooked

Salt and pepper to taste
1 teaspoon parsley, chopped
1 tablespoon onion, minced
2 tablespoons butter
2 tablespoons Parmesan
  cheese, grated

Place asparagus with garlic in water to cover and cook until tender. Remove garlic and discard, then drain asparagus, retaining 1 cup of juice. Bring chicken broth to boil, add chicken and rice, and simmer until rice is tender, about 30 minutes. Add remaining ingredients, asparagus, and cup of juice. Simmer about 10 minutes and serve hot.
Serves 6 to 8.

EGGPLANT SOUP

Zuppa Di Melanzana

1 small onion, chopped	2 cups beef stock
½ cup mushrooms, sliced	1 cup water
1 large tomato, quartered	1 teaspoon parsley, chopped
4 tablespoons olive oil	Salt and pepper to taste
1 medium eggplant, diced	

Fry onion, mushrooms, and tomatoes gently in olive oil for 5 minutes. Add remaining ingredients and bring to a boil quickly. Reduce heat, cover, and simmer about 30 minutes or until vegetables are tender. Sprinkle with freshly grated cheese if desired.
Serves 2 to 4.

SPINACH SOUP

Zuppa Di Spinaci

1 pound spinach, cleaned	¼ cup Romano or Pecorino
2 tablespoons onion, minced	cheese, grated
4 tablespoons olive oil	4 cups chicken broth
2 tablespoons butter	1 chicken breast, cooked and
Salt and pepper to taste	chopped
	2 eggs, beaten

Cook spinach in water to cover about 10 minutes, then drain. Fry onion gently in oil and butter, but do not brown. Add spinach, salt, pepper, and grated cheese. Fry gently about 5 minutes. Add chicken broth and chicken and bring to a boil. Add eggs, stirring briskly for a minute to make a lace effect. Simmer 5 minutes more and serve very hot.
Serves 4 to 6.

LENTIL SOUP

Zuppa Di Lenticchie

1 cup lentils
6 cups cold water
1 cup onion, minced
1 tablespoon olive oil

2-inch cube salt pork
1 clove garlic
Salt and pepper to taste
1 large tomato, chopped

Place lentils in water overnight. Brown onion in oil and fat from salt pork; add to lentils and water. Drop in garlic clove and cover. Simmer 1½ hours. Add salt, pepper, and tomato and simmer 10 more minutes. Remove garlic and serve.
Serves 6.

RICE SOUP

Zuppa Di Riso

2 quarts beef stock
1 small onion, chopped

Salt and pepper to taste
1 cup rice, uncooked

Bring beef stock to boil; add remaining ingredients. Cover and simmer 20 minutes or until rice is tender. Serve with freshly grated Italian cheese if desired.
Serves 2 to 4.

CHICK PEA SOUP

Zuppa Di Ceci

1 clove garlic, sliced
4 tablespoons olive oil
1 medium onion, chopped
2 cups ceci (chick peas),
    cooked

1 quart beef stock
Salt to taste
2-inch piece pepperoni sau-
    sage, sliced wafer thin

Brown garlic in olive oil, then remove and discard. Fry onion gently for 5 minutes, then add chick peas and beef stock. Add salt and sausage, cover, and simmer 30 to 40 minutes. Serve very hot.
Serves 4 to 6.

SALMON AND PEA SOUP

Zuppa Di Salmone E Piselli

1 small onion, minced
4 tablespoons olive oil
1 quart water
2 medium potatoes, minced
2 cups fresh green peas

Salt and pepper to taste
1 tablespoon parsley, chopped
Dash of oregano
2 cups canned pink salmon
½ cup light cream

Fry onion gently in olive oil about 5 minutes. Add water, potatoes, and peas; simmer until tender. Add salt, pepper, parsley, and oregano, and simmer about 10 minutes more. Add salmon and light cream, stir, and serve hot.
Serves 4 to 6.

Pasta

Did you ever go to Dough School? I did, and what marvelous teachers I had — my husband's mother, grandmothers, and aunts and all of his friends' relatives. It was an unusual school: Some of my instructors didn't speak English, and you didn't bring an apple for the teacher — you brought tomatoes. In addition to that, it was the only school I ever attended where my husband ate the homework.

Eventually I graduated with honors, but it certainly didn't start out that way. It's remarkable how a person of reasonable intelligence can suddenly turn into a "dum-dum" when it comes to handling dough. All that flour! I found that flour is very sneaky. Just when I thought I'd taken command, it would rebel. Flour has a way of attacking you when you're not looking, and not only you — it attacks the floor, the ceiling, and every flat surface within ten miles!

Dry it's bad enough — but *wet!* It was very difficult for me to get the dough to reach the proper consistency. I'd knead and pound and pray that it would come out right, and I threw away more balls of dough than an Italian bakery would in fifty years. When it finally worked I congratulated myself, but I wasn't finished yet. Now I had to stuff it.

Stuffing little pieces of dough with a moist mixture is a frustrating experience the first time around, and the second and probably the third. The filling oozes out the ends, slides through cracks, and ends up on your Mother Hubbard instead of staying obediently in its nice little roll, but there is a reward for all of this work. When you've finally achieved the desired result, it tastes like heaven. The most important thing to remember is that dough for pasta takes time and patience, so don't try to do it in a hurry.

My husband's mother and grandmother still make their own noodles. Imagine, every one of those tiny little strips is made by hand! However, manufactured noodle and pasta products are more than adequate for the recipes in this book, and I have only suggested my favorite sizes and shapes. There are dozens of other sizes and shapes to choose from, including the delicious imported ones, and they're all fun to use.

They're even more fun to eat.

Pasta Per Manicotti E Cannelloni

2 cups flour, sifted   ½ teaspoon salt
2 eggs   2 tablespoons water

Place flour on large pastry board, make hole in middle of flour, and drop in eggs, salt, and water. Beat eggs with fork, gradually mixing in half of flour. Mix rest of flour in with hands. Knead until dough is smooth and shape into large ball. Cut ball in half, and roll each half into paper-thin sheets. Cut dough in 4-inch squares. Cook about 4 squares at a time in large pot with boiling, salted water for 5 minutes. Remove from water one at a time and drain.
Fill as suggested below.
Makes about 2 dozen.

MANICOTTI STUFFED WITH CHEESE

Manicotti Imbottiti Con Ricotta

2 dozen prepared manicotti   4 eggs, beaten
2 pounds Ricotta cheese   Salt and pepper to taste
½ cup Romano cheese,   4 cups Tomato Sauce
   grated   Supreme (page 35)
2 tablespoons parsley,
   chopped

Have dough squares cooked, drained, and cooled. Thoroughly mix all ingredients except sauce. Spread about 2 tablespoons of this mixture on each square. Roll squares as tightly as possible without the filling coming out. Place 2 cups tomato sauce in large, shallow baking pan. Place manicotti side by side in pan. Pour remaining sauce on top. Bake in medium (350°F) oven for 30 minutes. Serve very hot.
Serves 6 to 8.

STUFFED PIPES

Cannelloni

2 dozen prepared cannelloni
1 clove garlic, minced
1 small onion, minced
2 tablespoons olive oil
1 cup chicken, cooked and
  minced

¼ pound prosciutto, minced
2 eggs, beaten
Salt and pepper to taste
1 cup Plain Tomato Sauce
  (page 34)
½ cup Romano cheese, grated

Have dough squares cooked, drained, and cooled. Brown garlic and onion slowly in oil until golden brown. Reduce heat. Add chicken and prosciutto and mix. Add eggs gradually with salt and pepper, stirring constantly. Heat slowly. Spread about 1 tablespoon of the mixture on each square. Roll as tightly as possible without the filling coming out. Place rolls in one layer in shallow greased baking pan. Coat with tomato sauce and sprinkle with cheese. Bake in medium (350°F) oven about 20 minutes or until cheese is golden. Serve very hot. *Serves 6 to 8.*

STUFFED NOODLES

Lasagne Imbottite

1 pound lasagne noodles
2 tablespoons olive oil
1 clove garlic, sliced
1 pound Italian sausage, cut
  into ¼-inch pieces
3 eggs, beaten
1 tablespoon parsley,
  chopped

½ teaspoon oregano
Salt and pepper to taste
3 cups Plain Tomato Sauce
  (page 34)
1 cup Romano cheese, grated
½ cup Mozzarella cheese,
  diced
1 pound Ricotta cheese

Boil noodles in salted water until tender, then drain. Heat oil and brown garlic, then remove and discard garlic. Brown sausage in oil. Mix beaten eggs with parsley, oregano, salt, and pepper, add to Ricotta and mix thoroughly. In large, shallow baking pan pour 1 cup tomato sauce. Place layer of noodles, layer of grated cheese, layer of sausage. Add another layer of tomato sauce and scatter Mozzarella and tablespoons of Ricotta here and there. Repeat until all ingredients are used. Pour remaining tomato sauce and grated cheese on top. Bake in medium (350°F) oven 30 minutes.
Serves 6 to 8.

RAVIOLI WITH MEAT STUFFING

Ravioli Con Carne

DOUGH

3 cups flour, sifted
2 eggs
2 tablespoons butter,
  softened

½ teaspoon salt
1 cup warm water

Place flour on pastry board; make hole in center of flour and drop in eggs, butter, and salt. Beat eggs with fork, gradually adding flour and water to make dough stiff. Knead with hands until smooth and shape into ball. Cut in half and roll each half on floured board until paper thin.

STUFFING

1 cup chicken, cooked and
  finely minced
½ cup prosciutto, minced
2 eggs, beaten
Salt and pepper to taste
1 teaspoon parsley, chopped

2 tablespoons Romano
  cheese, grated
1 cup spinach, cooked and
  chopped
2 tablespoons olive oil
4 cups Plain Tomato Sauce
  (page 34)

23

Mix all stuffing ingredients except tomato sauce into smooth paste. Place tablespoons of stuffing on a sheet of dough at 2-inch intervals. When sheet is filled with stuffing, cover with second sheet. Press around each mound with fingertips and cut in 2-inch squares with cutter. Close edges firmly so stuffing will not come out. Set aside on floured surface, not touching, and allow to stand about 30 minutes. Place ravioli 6 or 8 at a time in deep pot with boiling, salted water for 10 minutes. Remove with slotted spoon one at a time and place in warm bowl. Dot with spoonsful of hot tomato sauce. Repeat until all ravioli are cooked. Serve very hot with remaining sauce.
Serves 6 to 8.

RAVIOLI WITH CHEESE

Ravioli Con Ricotta

1 pound Ricotta cheese
½ cup Romano cheese, grated
2 tablespoons parsley, grated
2 eggs, beaten

Salt and pepper to taste
Prepared ravioli dough (page 23)
2 cups Tomato Sauce Supreme (page 35)

Mix first 5 ingredients thoroughly. Drop tablespoons of the mixture 2 inches apart on a sheet of dough. Cover with second sheet of dough and press around mounds with fingertips. Cut each ravioli with cutter; place on floured surface, not touching, and allow to stand about 30 minutes. Place ravioli, 6 or 8 at a time, in deep pot with boiling, salted water for 10 minutes. Remove with slotted spoon and place in warm bowl. Dot with spoonsful of sauce; repeat until all ravioli are cooked. Serve hot with remaining sauce.
Serves 6 to 8.

BAKED TUFOLI

Tufoli Al Forno

4 tablespoons olive oil
1 clove garlic, sliced
½ cup green onions, chopped
½ pound ground beef
½ pound ground veal
2 eggs, beaten
1 tablespoon parsley, chopped
⅛ teaspoon oregano

Salt and pepper to taste
1 pound tufoli, cooked and
  drained
4 cups Plain Tomato Sauce
  (page 34)
½ cup Romano cheese,
  grated

Heat oil in heavy skillet and brown garlic, then remove and discard garlic. Add onions, beef, and veal and brown lightly. Mix in next 4 ingredients. Stuff tufoli with meat mixture and place layer of tufoli in shallow, greased baking pan. Cover with layer of sauce and cheese; repeat until all ingredients are used. Cover and bake in medium (350°F) oven for 50 minutes. Serve very hot.
Serves 4 to 6.

SPAGHETTI WITH BROCCOLI

Spaghetti Con Broccoli

¼ cup olive oil
1 clove garlic, sliced
1 medium onion, chopped
2-pound can Italian tomatoes
1 tablespoon parsley, chopped
Dash of oregano
Salt and pepper to taste

2 bunches broccoli, cooked
  and cut in 1-inch pieces
1 pound spaghetti, cooked
  and drained
½ cup Romano cheese,
  grated

Heat oil in heavy skillet, brown garlic, then remove and discard garlic. Add onion to oil and fry gently until transparent.

Add tomatoes, parsley, oregano, salt, and pepper. Simmer 40 minutes, add broccoli, and simmer another 10 minutes. Mix well. Pour over hot spaghetti and sprinkle with grated cheese. Serve very hot.

Serves 2 to 4.

SPAGHETTI WITH EGGPLANT

Spaghetti Con Melanzana

½ cup olive oil
1 clove garlic, sliced
1 medium eggplant, cubed
1 green pepper, chopped
1-pound can Italian tomatoes

1 tablespoon parsley, chopped
Dash of oregano
Salt and pepper to taste
1 pound spaghetti

Heat oil in heavy skillet, brown garlic, then remove and discard garlic. Add eggplant and green pepper and brown lightly. Add tomatoes, parsley, oregano, salt, and pepper. Cover and simmer about 30 minutes. Cook spaghetti in boiling, salted water, drain, and place on large platter. Pour eggplant sauce over the top. Serve very hot.

Serves 2 to 4.

SPAGHETTI WITH SQUASH

Spaghetti Con Zucchini

2 medium zucchini, sliced
   about ⅛ inch thick
4 tablespoons olive oil
1 pound spaghetti

2 cups Plain Tomato Sauce
   (page 34)
½ cup Pecorino cheese,
   grated
Salt and pepper to taste

Fry zucchini in oil until golden brown, remove, and drain. Cook spaghetti until tender, drain, and place on large platter. Place zucchini over spaghetti and cover with sauce, cheese, salt, and pepper. Serve very hot.
Serves 4 to 6.

NOODLES WITH CHEESE AND SAUSAGE

Fettuccine Con Formaggio E Salsiccia

¼ cup olive oil	1 pound fettuccine
1 clove garlic, sliced	1 cup Ricotta cheese
6-ounce can tomato paste	½ cup Mozzarella cheese, diced
3 Italian sausages, sweet or hot, chopped	½ cup Romano cheese, grated
1 tablespoon parsley, chopped	2 tablespoons breadcrumbs
Salt and pepper to taste	

Heat oil in large, heavy skillet. Brown garlic, then remove and discard. Add tomato paste to oil and fry gently until bubbly. Fill tomato paste can with water and add to skillet; add sausages, parsley, salt, and pepper. Simmer about 50 minutes. Boil egg noodles in salted water until tender, then drain. Put in deep bowl, add cheeses and sausages with all but ½ cup of sauce, and mix thoroughly. Spread breadcrumbs in greased baking dish. Pour noodles with sauce into dish, top with extra ½ cup sauce, and bake in medium (350°F) oven for 30 minutes.
Serves 4 to 6.

Rigatoni Con Salsiccia

1 pound Italian sausage,
    sweet or hot
1/4 cup olive oil
1 clove garlic, sliced thin
1 medium onion, chopped
2 cups mushrooms, sliced
6-ounce can tomato paste

6-ounce can water
1/4 teaspoon oregano
1 tablespoon parsley, chopped
Salt and pepper to taste
1 pound rigatoni
1/4 cup Romano cheese,
    grated

Brown sausage on all sides in hot skillet. Remove, drain, and cut in 1-inch pieces. Add oil to pan, add garlic, onion, and mushrooms and fry gently about 10 minutes. Add sausage, tomato paste, water, oregano, parsley, salt, and pepper. Cover and simmer 1 hour. Boil rigatoni until tender but not too soft, and place in greased baking dish. Pour sausage mixture on top. Sprinkle grated cheese over sauce and bake in medium (350°F) oven 15 minutes or until cheese is browned and bubbling. Serve very hot.
Serves 4 to 6.

Capellini Con Acciughe

1/4 cup olive oil
1 clove garlic, sliced
1 medium onion, minced
1-pound can Italian tomatoes
Salt and pepper to taste

Dash of oregano
1 tablespoon parsley, chopped
2-ounce can anchovy fillets,
    chopped
1 pound capellini

Heat oil in heavy skillet and brown garlic, then remove garlic and discard. Fry onion gently until golden. Add tomatoes,

salt, pepper, oregano, and parsley. Simmer 10 minutes. Add anchovies; cover and simmer 1 hour. Cook capellini in boiling, salted water until tender, then drain. Place on large platter and pour sauce over top. Serve hot.
Serves 2 to 4.

MACARONI AND BEANS

Pasta E Fagioli

1/4 cup olive oil	1 tablespoon parsley, chopped
2 cloves garlic, sliced	1 cup Ditali, small shells, or
1 large onion, diced	small elbow macaroni
1-pound can Italian tomatoes	2 cups canned cannellini or
Salt and pepper to taste	red kidney beans,
1/4 teaspoon oregano	undrained

Heat oil in large, heavy skillet. Fry garlic until brown, then discard. Fry onions slowly until soft. Add tomatoes, salt, pepper, oregano, and parsley. Simmer 30 minutes. Cook macaroni until just tender, then drain. Add macaroni and beans to tomato mixture and simmer over low heat about 5 minutes more. Serve hot.
Serves 4.

MACARONI WITH CHICK PEAS

Pasta Con Ceci

1 cup Ditalini	1 clove garlic
2 cups chick peas, cooked	Salt and pepper to taste
4 or 5 slices bacon	

Cook Ditalini until almost tender, drain, and save 2 cups juice. Place Ditalini and juice in pot with chick peas. Fry bacon with garlic until crisp. Remove bacon and garlic and pour bacon grease over Ditalini and lentils. Add salt and pepper. Simmer until Ditalini is tender. Serve with bacon crumbled over top.
Serves 2 to 4.

MACARONI WITH LENTILS

Pasta Con Lenticchie

1 cup Ditalini
2 cups lentils, cooked
4 or 5 slices bacon

1 clove garlic
Salt and pepper to taste

Cook Ditalini until almost tender, drain, and save 2 cups juice. Place Ditalini and juice in pot with lentils. Fry bacon with garlic until crisp. Remove bacon and garlic and pour bacon grease over Ditalini and lentils. Add salt and pepper. Simmer until Ditalini is tender. Serve with bacon crumbled over top.
Serves 2 to 4.

MACARONI WITH BROCCOLI DI RAPPI

Pasta Con Broccoli Di Rappi

2 bunches broccoli di rappi,
  cleaned
1 cup Ditalini

4 or 5 slices bacon
1 clove garlic
Salt to taste

Place broccoli in pot with boiling water. Cook until almost tender and drain. Cook Ditalini until almost done and drain,

saving 2 cups of the juice. Add to broccoli with enough of this juice to cover and cook together until done. Fry bacon with garlic until crisp. Remove bacon and garlic and pour bacon grease over broccoli and Ditalini. Add salt. Serve with bacon crumbled over top .
Serves 4 to 6.

Note: Broccoli di rappi is thin, tender Italian broccoli. Regular broccoli may be used in the same manner.

BAKED RICE WITH SAUSAGE

Riso Con Salsiccia Al Forno

4 tablespoons olive oil
1 medium onion, minced
¾ pound Italian sausage, chopped
1 cup fresh green peas

½ cup mushrooms, sliced
1 cup beef stock
3 cups rice, cooked
½ cup Romano cheese, grated

Heat oil in large skillet, and brown onion, sausage, and **peas.** Add mushrooms and ½ cup beef stock; stir. Cover and simmer 25 minutes, then stir in rice and remaining stock. **Mix** and place in greased casserole. Sprinkle cheese on top and bake in medium (350°F) oven 30 minutes.
Serves 4.

WINE-FLAVORED RICE

Riso Al Vino

⅔ cup butter
1 small onion, minced
½ clove garlic, minced
2 pimientos, cut in strips

2 cups rice, uncooked
Beef stock as needed
1 cup Romano cheese, grated
¼ cup dry sherry

Melt half the butter in a skillet and gently fry onion and garlic in it until golden brown. Add pimientos and rice. Add a little beef stock and simmer, stirring constantly. Add more stock as needed for about 20 minutes. Rice should be cooked by then. Add remaining butter, cheese, and sherry. Mix thoroughly. Serve very hot.

Serves 4.

POTATO DUMPLINGS

Gnocchi Di Patate

2½ cups potatoes, boiled and
   mashed
½ teaspoon salt
2 eggs, beaten

2¼ cups flour
4 cups Tomato Sauce
   Supreme (page 35)
1 cup Romano cheese, grated

Mix potatoes, salt, and eggs in bowl. Add 1½ cups flour and mix well. Place dough on floured pastry board, add rest of flour, and knead about 5 minutes. Roll dough into long, rope-like strips about ¾ inch thick. Cut into ¾-inch long pieces. Sprinkle with flour and make mark by pressing down with fork in middle of each piece. Boil in at least 8 quarts salted water until they rise to the top, about 10 minutes. Drain and serve with tomato sauce and cheese.

Serves 4 to 6.

Sauces

When I was still living at home and my mother cooked, there were only certain things she had to do — say, to a roast of beef. She'd rub a little salt and pepper on it, stick a meat thermometer in it, and, if she was really daring, throw some peppercorns and herbs over the top; then she'd slide it into the oven and wait. Well, tomato sauce is different — very different. So are the instructions you get on how to put it together.

My first attempt at sauce, before some kind people helped me, was a disaster. I assembled what I thought were the right ingredients, surrounded myself with a pile of Italian cookbooks, and locked the door. There are a lot of myths about preparing Italian sauce. One of them is that you have to stay in the kitchen all day, looking worried and yelling, *"Mamma Mia!"* Another is that you *must* remove the seeds from the tomatoes! Well, I took that one seriously. Believe it or not, I spent the whole afternoon tediously separating seeds from tomatoes! Then I strained and re-strained the empty tomatoes. At dinnertime I had nothing more to show for my labors than a dish of seeds and some rather tired-looking tomato juice.

Upon discovering my tomato fiasco, my long-suffering husband gallantly remarked that he hadn't had homemade tomato juice in a long time. He also suggested that if I looked hard enough, I'd probably find a recipe for tomato seed patties somewhere.

The following sauce recipes are myth-proof, but if you still want to take out the seeds, go ahead.

PLAIN TOMATO SAUCE

Salsa Di Pomodoro Semplice

½ cup olive oil
2 large onions, cut up
2 cloves garlic, sliced
2-pound can Italian tomatoes,
    strained

Salt and pepper to taste
1 tablespoon parsley, chopped
¼ teaspoon oregano
1 bay leaf

Heat oil in large, heavy skillet, then brown the onions and garlic. When they are golden brown, remove from oil and discard. Add the tomatoes to the oil, cover, and simmer over low heat for 50 minutes. Stir occasionally. Add the salt, pepper, parsley, oregano, and bay leaf. Cover and simmer about 20 minutes more. Remove bay leaf and discard.
Makes about 3½ cups sauce.

TOMATO SAUCE SUPREME

Salsa Di Pomodoro Supremo

1/4 cup olive oil
2 cloves garlic, sliced
2 medium onions, sliced
12-ounce can tomato paste
1-pound can Italian tomatoes

2 cups cold water
Salt and pepper to taste
Dash of oregano
1 tablespoon parsley, chopped

In large, heavy skillet heat olive oil. Add garlic and onions and fry slowly. When golden brown, remove from oil and discard. Add tomato paste to hot oil and fry gently for 5 minutes. Add tomatoes and water and stir. Add salt, pepper, oregano, and parsley. Cover and simmer slowly 1 to 2 hours until sauce is thick.
Makes about 5 cups sauce.

SICILIAN SAUCE

Salsa Alla Siciliana

1 large onion, minced
1 large clove garlic, minced
1/4 cup olive oil
2 12-ounce cans tomato paste
6 12-ounce cans water
1/2 teaspoon oregano
1 teaspoon sweet basil

1/2 teaspoon sugar
1/8 teaspoon cinnamon
Dash of allspice
Salt and pepper to taste
1/4 cup Romano cheese,
  grated

Slowly fry onion and garlic in oil until tender. Add tomato paste and stir until well blended, then add water and stir. Add the seasonings and simmer uncovered until thickened, about 2 hours. Before serving, sprinkle the cheese into the sauce and mix thoroughly.
Makes about 1 quart sauce.

Salsa Con Carne

4 tablespoons olive oil
1 clove garlic, sliced
1 small onion, diced
½ pound ground beef
1-pound can tomato puree

Salt and pepper to taste
1 tablespoon parsley, chopped
Dash of oregano
½ cup water

Heat oil in large, heavy skillet, add garlic, and fry slowly. When golden brown, remove garlic and discard. Add onion and beef to hot oil and cook slowly until onion is transparent; do not let it burn. Add puree, salt, pepper, parsley, oregano, and water. Cover and simmer about 1½ hours. *Makes about 2½ cups sauce.*

MEAT AND MUSHROOM SAUCE

Salsa Con Carne E Funghi

¼ cup olive oil
2 cloves garlic, sliced
1 cup mushrooms, sliced
½ pound ground pork
½ pound ground veal

2-pound can Italian tomatoes, strained
6-ounce can tomato paste
Salt and pepper to taste

Heat oil in large, heavy skillet or saucepan. Add garlic and fry slowly. When golden brown, remove garlic and discard. Add mushrooms, pork, and veal and simmer for 10 minutes. Add tomatoes, cover, and simmer 50 minutes, stirring occasionally. Add tomato paste, salt, and pepper and mix thoroughly. Cover and simmer about 35 minutes more. *Makes about 4 cups sauce.*

TUNA SAUCE

Salsa Con Tonno

1 clove garlic, sliced
1/4 cup olive oil
12-ounce can tomato paste
1 or 2 7 1/2-ounce cans white
   chunk tuna

Salt and pepper to taste
Dash of oregano
1 tablespoon parsley, chopped
1 1/2 cups water

Brown garlic in hot oil; when crisp, remove and discard. Add tomato paste and fry gently about 5 minutes. Add tuna, salt, pepper, oregano, parsley, and water. Cover and simmer 30 minutes. Bring to a fast boil and immediately reduce heat. If sauce is too thick, add a little more water and simmer another 10 minutes.
Makes about 3 cups sauce.

CLAM SAUCE

Salsa Con Vongole

1/4 cup olive oil
2 cloves garlic, sliced
2-pound can Italian tomatoes
1/2 teaspoon salt
Black pepper to taste
Dash of oregano

2 tablespoons parsley,
   chopped
1 dozen medium-sized fresh
   clams, cut up (or 1 or 2
   7 1/2-ounce cans minced
   clams)

Heat oil in large, heavy skillet. Add garlic and fry slowly until golden brown, then remove and discard. Add tomatoes, salt, pepper, oregano, and parsley. Cover and simmer for 50 minutes. Add clams with their juices and simmer another 5 minutes. Do not overcook clams.
Makes about 3 1/2 cups sauce.

OIL AND GARLIC WHITE SAUCE

Salsa Bianca Di Olio E Aglio

½ cup olive oil
2 cloves garlic, sliced
½ cup water
½ teaspoon salt

Black pepper to taste
2 tablespoons parsley,
  chopped
Dash of oregano

Heat oil in large, heavy skillet. Add garlic and brown, being careful not to burn it. When golden brown, remove from oil and discard. Add remaining ingredients and simmer for 15 minutes. Serve at once.
Makes about 1 cup sauce.

Note: Clams or tuna may be added to this recipe.

BUTTER AND CHEESE SAUCE

Salsa Di Burro E Formaggio

¾ pound butter
1 small onion, minced
1 clove garlic, minced
1 tablespoon parsley, chopped
Dash of oregano

Salt and pepper to taste
¼ teaspoon paprika
¼ cup Romano cheese,
  freshly grated

Melt butter in saucepan, but do not burn. Sauté onion and garlic in butter until transparent. Add parsley, oregano, salt, pepper, and paprika. Stir and simmer slowly about 10 minutes, then add cheese, stirring constantly. Turn off heat and serve at once.
Makes about 1 cup sauce.

Seafood

I've shared all my problems with you thus far, so I'll have to be honest about everything. I did have a few apprehensive moments with some of the seafoods, especially one — lumache. "That's snails, lady, snails!" Friends graciously gave me their recipes, but even while I was writing them down I was terrified. I didn't even think I could get the snails home without them attacking me, not to mention turning them into a masterpiece.

I haven't felt too ashamed of my reluctance to handle some of the more exotic creatures of the sea since my mother-in-law told me of her childhood aversion to lobsters. When she was sent to purchase live lobsters for the family dinner, she wouldn't start the journey home until she had tied a length of ribbon around the bag. She would then drag the bag behind her like a pull toy. Now this is a real, live Italian, and if she was afraid of a lobster I can admit to being scared of snails. Of course my mother-in-law was only ten at the time.

Well, one day I bravely decided to make the best snails my husband ever ate. I put them in water to soak overnight as directed, plunked the stone on the lid of the pot, and went to bed. I didn't sleep much that night. I kept wondering if snails get claustrophobia and if they would resent my opening their little "door" in the morning. Now I believe that a man's home is his castle, and I feel that a snail has the same right. It just didn't seem fair to go barging through that door, poking into their little house. I suppose you could say the same thing about a clam or an oyster, but somehow their shells look as though they were meant to be opened — a snail's is all curled up, as if he's trying to hide.

I had quite a day! I scrubbed and rinsed and drained, then I rinsed and soaked and drained some more. With each succeeding soak, drain, and rinse my husband's appetite was sharpening, and I was becoming more familiar with the little devils. I was even beginning to feel a bit sorry for them and their involuntary bathing, although they didn't resent my intrusion; they were all at home and they cooperated beautifully. The snails were delicious the first time.

I don't have much to say about eels and squid — you either like them or you don't, and if you do, there's a recipe for each.

None of the recipes in this chapter is particularly difficult; all can be turned into delicious meals. Just be sure to follow the directions carefully, and you can start enjoying the sea Italian style.

Vongole Crude Con Salsa Bianca

4 dozen small clams, scrubbed   1 teaspoon parsley, minced
4 tablespoons olive oil   Dash of oregano
Juice from 2 fresh lemons   1 teaspoon green onions,
Salt and pepper to taste   finely minced

Open clams with clam knife (twist knife to force shells apart) and cut clam loose from shell. Drain off juice and reserve it, leaving clam in its larger shell. Place clams on large platter over ice. Combine juice with remaining ingredients and blend well, using mixture as a dip for clams. Serve well chilled.
Serves 4.

STEAMED CLAMS

Vongole Fumante

2 tablespoons olive oil   1 cup water
1 clove garlic, halved   Salt and pepper to taste
2 tablespoons parsley,   4 dozen small clams,
  chopped   scrubbed

Heat oil, garlic, and parsley in deep pot for 5 minutes. Add water, salt, pepper, and clams. Cover and steam gently 20 minutes or until clams open. Serve with clam broth.
Serves 4.

SHRIMP WITH MUSHROOMS

Gamberetti Con Funghi

1 clove garlic, sliced	2 eggs, beaten
1/4 cup olive oil	1/2 cup flour
2 cups mushrooms, sliced	Salt and pepper to taste
2 pounds large shrimp, shelled and deveined	1/2 cup dry white wine

Brown garlic lightly in oil, then discard. Add mushrooms to oil and sauté about 5 minutes. Remove from oil and keep warm. Dip shrimp in eggs, then roll in flour, salt, and pepper. Fry shrimp gently in oil until golden brown. Add mushrooms and wine and cook over high heat 5 minutes or until wine is evaporated. Serve very hot.
Serves 2 to 4.

SHRIMP AND NOODLES

Gamberetti E Linguini

1 pound raw shrimp, shelled and deveined	2 cups Plain Tomato Sauce (page 34)
1 medium onion, minced	1/2 cup dry white wine
1/4 cup green pepper, minced	Salt and pepper to taste
1 clove garlic, minced	1/4 teaspoon allspice
1/4 cup olive oil	1 pound linguini, cooked

Boil shrimp and drain. Fry onion, green pepper, and garlic gently in oil for 10 minutes. Add next 4 ingredients and simmer 30 minutes. Add shrimp and heat thoroughly. Pour over hot linguini and serve.
Serves 4 to 6.

STUFFED LOBSTER

Aragosta Imbottita

1 large lobster, boiled and cut in half	Salt and pepper to taste
8 large mushroom stems, minced	2 cups of any meatless tomato sauce
1 clove garlic, minced	8 large mushroom caps
1 very small onion, minced	1 tablespoon butter
3 tablespoons olive oil	1/4 cup Romano cheese, grated
1 teaspoon parsley, chopped	

Remove lobster meat from shell, keeping claw meat separate; save shells. Separate mushroom caps from stems. Lightly brown garlic, onion, minced mushroom stems, and chopped claw meat in hot oil. Add lobster meat, parsley, salt, and pepper and 1 cup tomato sauce. Mix and simmer 5 minutes. Fill shell halves with mixture and place in shallow baking pan. Arrange mushroom caps around lobster and dot with butter. Pour remaining tomato sauce over lobster and around mushrooms. Sprinkle with grated cheese and bake in medium (350°F) oven for 20 minutes.
Serves 2.

SNAILS WITH MARINER SAUCE

Lumache Con Salsa Marinara

SNAILS

5 pounds live snails	10 tablespoons salt

Place snails in deep, covered pot and soak in plain water overnight. Place stone or heavy object on lid so snails can't crawl out. Drain. Open "door" end of shells, put in fresh

43

water for 5 minutes, and drain. Do not use any snails that
don't emerge from shells. Rinse and scrub each shell until
clean. Return to deep pot and cover with water to 5 or 6
inches above snails. Add 2 tablespoons salt. Do not overuse
salt or snails will burn. Soak 15 to 20 minutes, then drain.
Repeat soaking, salting, and draining process 3 more times.
Add fresh water and remaining 2 tablespoons salt, cover, and
put over low heat. When water starts to boil, turn up heat
and boil 45 minutes. Remove foam from top of water, drain,
and rinse in cool water. Save 1 cup of broth for sauce.

SAUCE

1/4 cup olive oil
1 clove garlic, sliced
1 medium onion, chopped
6-ounce can tomato paste
1-pound can Italian tomatoes
1/2 cup water

1 cup broth from snails
Salt and pepper to taste
1 tablespoon parsley, chopped
1/2 teaspoon crushed red
  pepper (optional)

Heat oil and brown garlic and onion. When golden brown,
remove and discard. Add tomato paste to oil and fry gently
until bubbling, stirring constantly. Add tomatoes, water, and
broth from snails and stir. Add salt, pepper, and parsley.
Cover and simmer 25 minutes. Return snails to deep pot,
pour sauce over them, and simmer for 30 minutes, stirring
frequently. For hot sauce, add crushed red peppers. Serve
very hot in soup dish.
Serves 4.

STUFFED SQUID SILBA

Calamai Imbottiti Alla Silba

SQUID

2 pounds squid
2 cups Italian breadcrumbs
Salt and pepper to taste

1 teaspoon parsley, chopped
5 tablespoons sauce (page 45)

44

Peel filmlike bluish skin from squid. Separate tentacles from body by pulling apart. Remove V-shaped spine from body. Turn body inside out and clean. After cleaning, turn body rightside out again. Turn tentacles back and clean; remove eyes. Mix breadcrumbs, salt, pepper, parsley, and sauce. Stuff body and close open end with toothpick. If mixture is too dry, add a little more sauce.

SAUCE

½ cup olive oil

2 6-ounce cans tomato paste

2 2-pound cans Italian peeled tomatoes, strained

Salt and pepper to taste

Heat oil and fry tomato paste gently until bubbling. Add tomatoes, salt, and pepper. Stir and simmer for 45 minutes. Add stuffed squid and simmer for 45 minutes more.

TOPPING

1 cup Italian breadcrumbs

3 tablespoons olive oil

Fry breadcrumbs in oil over low flame in skillet until crisp and golden, stirring constantly. Sprinkle over squid nd sauce before serving.

Serves 4 to 6.

FRIED EELS

Capitone Fritto

1 cup Italian breadcrumbs

Salt and pepper to taste

½ teaspoon paprika

1 eel, about 3 pounds, cleaned

1 egg, beaten

¼ cup olive oil

Mix breadcrumbs, salt, pepper, and paprika. Cut eel into 2-inch pieces, dip first into egg, then into crumb mixture. Fry in hot oil until golden brown. Serve very hot.

Serves 4 to 6.

CODFISH WITH HOT DRY PEPPERS

Baccalà Con Pepe Forte

1-pound dried, salted codfish   1/4 cup olive oil
2 hot, dried cherry peppers

Soak codfish in water overnight, then drain. Add fresh water to cover and boil gently until tender. Drain and add fresh cold water to cover; allow to sit about 1 hour, then drain again. Break into bite-sized chunks. Break peppers into pieces and fry slowly over low heat in olive oil for 15 minutes. Add codfish and heat thoroughly for 10 minutes.
Serves 2 to 4.

HELEN'S CODFISH SALAD

Insalata Di Baccalà Alla Elena

2-pound dried, salted codfish   3 cloves garlic, chopped
1/4 cup olive oil   Black pepper to taste
Juice from 1 fresh lemon   3 sprigs fresh parsley

Soak codfish in water overnight, then drain. Add fresh water to cover and boil gently until tender. Drain and add fresh cold water to cover; allow to sit about 1 hour, then drain again. Separate into bite-sized chunks with fork. Blend oil,

lemon juice, garlic, pepper, and parsley. Pour mixture over codfish and chill. Serve cold.
Serves 4 to 6.

BAKED FLOUNDER

Pesce Al Forno

4-pound flounder, cleaned	*⅛ teaspoon paprika*
Salt and pepper to taste	*½ cup olive oil*
¼ teaspoon oregano	*½ cup dry white wine*

Place fish in shallow, greased baking dish. Blend salt, pepper, oregano, paprika, and olive oil. Pour over fish and bake in medium (350°F) oven for 30 minutes. During the last 10 minutes, pour wine over fish. Serve very hot.
Serves 4 to 6.

BREADED HADDOCK

Pesce Panato

1 clove garlic, chopped	*2 tablespoons parsley,*
½ cup olive oil	*chopped*
1 cup Italian breadcrumbs	*Salt and pepper to taste*
½ cup Romano cheese,	*2 pounds haddock fillets*
grated	*2 eggs, beaten*

Brown garlic lightly in oil, then discard. Mix breadcrumbs, cheese, parsley, salt, and pepper. Dip fish first into eggs, then into crumb mixture. Drop in hot oil and fry until crisp and golden. Serve very hot.
Serves 2 to 4.

47

BOILED WHITING

Merluzzo Lesso

1½ pounds of whiting,
  cleaned
1½ cups water
½ cup dry white wine
1 clove garlic, halved

1 teaspoon parsley, chopped
1 bay leaf
1 very small onion, whole
Salt and pepper to taste

Place fish in pot with water and all other ingredients. Bring to a boil quickly, then reduce heat and simmer for 30 minutes. Serve very hot with the broth.
Serves 2 to 4.

UNCLE BENNY'S FISH STEW

Umido Di Pesce Zio Benedict

½ cup olive oil
1 large green pepper,
  chopped
3 shallots, chopped
3 cloves garlic, sliced thin
2 medium onions, quartered
1-pound can Italian tomatoes
3½ cups water
¼ teaspoon marjoram
½ cup parsley, chopped
1 teaspoon oregano

1 teaspoon basil
1 cup burgundy
1 cup sauterne
Salt and pepper to taste
6 large lobster claws in shells
2 dozen large shrimp in shells
3 dozen small clams,
  scrubbed
2 pounds whiting, cut in
  3-inch pieces

Heat oil in heavy skillet and fry green pepper, shallots, garlic, and onions until lightly browned. Add tomatoes and water. Cover and simmer 20 minutes. Add marjoram, parsley, oregano, and basil. Simmer for 5 minutes more. Add wines,

salt, and pepper. Cover and cook slowly 1 hour. Place lobster claws, shrimp, and clams in large, deep pot and top with fish. Pour sauce over all, cover, and simmer 30 minutes or until clams have opened. Serve very hot.
Serves 6 to 8.

SALMON SALAD

Insalata Di Salmone

1 pound canned salmon	*Black pepper to taste*
4 large tomatoes, quartered	*½ cup green onions, chopped*
½ clove garlic, minced	*Olive oil to taste*
Dash of basil	

Drain salmon and break into chunks. Mix all other ingredients gently in large bowl. Place salmon in bowl with mixture, cover, and chill thoroughly. When ready to serve, gently mix salad together.
Serves 2 to 4.

meats and Game

I'm sure steak purists would faint if they saw my husband's family handle that cut of meat. Purists believe that only butter — and sometimes not even that — should be added to the steak, which has been held with velvet-tipped tongs and cooked by a chef wearing a surgical mask, finally coming to rest on a shockproof, insulated platter. Not the Italians! They handle their steaks with great gusto. First comes the oil marinade, next the garlic, then any particular spice that might appeal to their imagination. After these preliminary preparations, it's gleefully picked up with a fork and thrown into a red-hot skillet. There it sizzles and spatters until it's done. Oh, the aroma! The taste cannot be equaled anywhere. I know. And I used to be a steak purist.

Now about meatballs. What can you do wrong to a little ball of meat? That depends upon what recipe you use. After my every endeavor, my poor husband would shake his head at me pityingly; I thought I'd *never* get them right. There are so many ways to make meatballs. Some people use only beef, some use pork and veal, some use pork and veal and beef. Some families like meatballs hard; my husband likes them soft. Some cooks use breadcrumbs and some use pieces of Italian bread that have been soaked in hot water, then squeezed out. Some brown the meatballs before they go into the sauce, some put raw meatballs into the sauce to cook, some make little meatballs, some make big meatballs. I felt like a meatball myself by the time I perfected mine.

Italians can be very creative when it comes to meat. The recipe I'm most proud of is Brain on Hot Coals, which was my husband's grandfather's favorite. In fact, my husband thinks his grandfather invented it. He knows it's quite old because it was cooked on hot coals when they were a necessity and not a backyard luxury. I know one thing; if you make it in your backyard, don't let the aroma carry too far or you'll have a lot of unexpected guests.

Most cuts of meat in this chapter will be familiar to you; the ones that aren't can easily be purchased in any Italian food store.

Bistecca Alla Scaloni

2-pound top round steak,   Dash of oregano
  ¾ inch thick   Dash of parsley
4 tablespoons olive oil   Salt and pepper to taste
2 cloves garlic, sliced   ¼ cup water

Place steak whole or in serving pieces on large platter. Coat with oil on both sides. Mash garlic on steak with fork. Add oregano, parsley, salt, and pepper to both sides. Pierce meat in spots with fork so that oil and seasonings go through. Allow to sit about 1½ hours, turning occasionally. Heat heavy skillet until almost red hot; remove garlic and discard. Drop steak into hot skillet and fry to desired stage of doneness; place on hot platter. Add water to skillet to make juice, and pour over steak before serving. Serve very hot.
Serves 4.

STEAK WITH CHEESE

Bistecca Con Mozzarella

4-pound beef round steak,   1 clove garlic, halved
  cut ½ inch thick   1 cup green pepper, chopped
¾ cup flour   4 cups Italian tomatoes
4 tablespoons olive oil   ¼ cup onions, minced
Salt and pepper to taste   ½ pound Mozzarella cheese,
2 cups water   sliced thin

Cut meat into 8 pieces. Roll in ½ cup flour. Brown in hot oil and remove to shallow baking pan. Blend remaining flour with hot drippings. Add salt and pepper; gradually add

water. Add garlic, green pepper, tomatoes, and onions. Cook, stirring until slightly thickened. Pour over meat and bake, covered, in medium (350°F) oven for 2½ hours or until meat is tender. Place slices of cheese on top and return to oven until cheese melts.
Serves 6 to 8.

ROLLED STEAK

Bistecca Braciola

1 large clove garlic, sliced very thin
¼ cup Romano cheese, grated
2 tablespoons parsley, chopped

Salt and pepper to taste
1½-pound slice of round steak, about ¾ inch thick
Any tomato sauce

Mix garlic, cheese, parsley, salt, and pepper. Spread over one side of steak. Roll and tie firmly with string so that stuffing doesn't fall out. Place in sauce of your choice to cover and simmer about 2 hours. Slice in ½-inch slices and serve very hot.

VARIATION
Prepare as above, but without sauce. Brown in hot fat on all sides. Place in casserole and cover. Bake in medium (350°F) oven about 2 hours. Slice in ½-inch slices and serve very hot.
Serves 2 to 4.

ROLLED CUBE STEAK

Braciuolini Di Manzo Scasciatta

1½-pound cube steak, about
  ½ inch thick
1 large clove garlic, sliced
  thin
¼ cup Romano cheese,
  grated

2 tablespoons parsley,
  chopped
¼ teaspoon oregano
Salt and pepper to taste
4 tablespoons olive oil

Cut steak into serving pieces. Mix all remaining ingredients, except olive oil, and spread mixture on one side of each piece of steak. Roll with mixture on inside and tie with string. Brown on all sides in hot olive oil, then place in shallow baking dish. Cover and bake in medium (350°F) oven 1 hour. Serve very hot.
Serves 2 to 4.

JUDY'S CUBE STEAK

Manzo Scasciatta Alla Gudizia

2 tablespoons olive oil
1 clove garlic, mashed
1 3-pound slice of cube steak
1 cup water

3 green peppers, sliced
½ pound mushrooms, whole
Salt and pepper to taste

Heat oil in heavy skillet; add garlic and steak and brown very quickly on both sides. Add water, green peppers, mushrooms, salt, and pepper. Cover and simmer until tender. Serve very hot.
Serves 4.

Polpette

3 pounds ground beef, pork,
and veal, mixed
2 cloves garlic, minced
2 eggs, beaten
¼ cup breadcrumbs

¼ cup Romano cheese,
grated
¼ teaspoon oregano
2 tablespoons parsley, minced
Salt and pepper to taste

Mix all ingredients thoroughly. Shape into 1½- to 2-inch balls. These may be browned in oil before going into desired sauce or they may be put into sauce raw. These meatballs may also be baked in medium (350°F) oven 1 hour without sauce.
Makes about 24 meatballs.

Note: To make softer meatballs, add water while mixing to desired consistency.

MEATBALLS ALLA LUCY

Polpette Alla Lucia

1 pound ground beef
1 pound ground pork
1 clove garlic, minced
½ teaspoon oregano
½ cup Romano or Parmesan
cheese, grated

2 tablespoons fresh parsley,
chopped
Salt and pepper to taste
2 eggs, beaten
¼ cup olive oil

Mix beef and pork; add all remaining ingredients but oil and mix thoroughly. Shape into balls about 2 inches in diameter. Fry in oil until lightly browned and remove. Make sauce of your choice in same oil. When sauce is ready to simmer, drop meatballs into it. They may cook as long as sauce does.
Makes about 24 meatballs.

MEATBALL CASSEROLE
Casseruola Di Polpette

1 pound ground beef
1 pound ground pork
1 clove garlic, minced
½ teaspoon oregano
1 cup Romano cheese, grated
2 tablespoons parsley,
  chopped
2 eggs, beaten
Salt and pepper to taste
½ cup olive oil

1 medium onion, sliced
3 carrots, quartered
3 medium potatoes,
  quartered
1 teaspoon basil
1 medium green pepper,
  sliced
½ cup Pecorino cheese,
  grated

Mix first 8 ingredients thoroughly. Roll meatballs and place in baking dish. Add next 6 ingredients, cover, and bake 1 hour in medium (350°F) oven. Before serving, sprinkle top with Pecorino cheese and serve very hot.
Serves 6 to 8.

MEAT LOAF
Polpettone

6-ounce can tomato paste
6-ounce can water
3 pounds ground beef or
  mixed beef, veal, and pork
Salt and pepper to taste
¼ cup olive oil
3 eggs

¼ cup Romano cheese,
  grated
¼ cup breadcrumbs
1 tablespoon parsley, chopped
1 green pepper, chopped
1 medium onion, chopped

Mix tomato paste and water until smooth. Divide in half. Thoroughly mix remaining ingredients with half of sauce mixture. Place in loaf pan, pour remaining sauce over top,

and bake in medium (350°F) oven for 2 hours. Serve hot.
Serves 4 to 6.

MEAT LOAF WITH RICOTTA

Polpettone Con Ricotta

½ pound ground beef
½ pound ground veal
1 cup breadcrumbs
¼ cup water
2 tablespoons parsley, chopped
4 eggs

¼ cup Romano cheese, grated
1 medium onion, minced
1 clove garlic, minced
Salt and pepper to taste
1 pound Ricotta cheese
3 tablespoons olive oil

Mix together meat, breadcrumbs, water, 1 tablespoon parsley, 2 eggs, Romano cheese, onion, garlic, salt, and pepper. In separate bowl mix Ricotta with remaining eggs and parsley until well blended. Coat baking dish with half the oil and put half the meat in dish; spread cheese mixture over entire surface. Place rest of meat on top and close edges so cheese mixture doesn't fall out. Coat with remaining oil and bake 30 minutes in medium (350°F) oven or until Ricotta is set and meat is brown but not dry.
Serves 6 to 8.

BAKED VEAL CHOPS

Costolette Di Vitello Al Forno

4 loin veal chops
4 tablespoons prosciutto, chopped
4 tablespoons Parmesan cheese, grated

Salt and pepper to taste
2 cups Meat Sauce (page 36)

Place veal chops in baking dish. Place 1 tablespoon prosciutto and cheese on each. Add salt and pepper. Push meat sauce through sieve and pour around chops. Bake in medium (350°F) oven 1 hour. Serve very hot.
Serves 4.

VEAL CUTLETS ALLA DANTE

Cotolette Di Vitello Alla Dante

2 pounds veal cutlets,
 ½ inch thick
1 clove garlic, sliced
Salt and pepper to taste

Dash of parsley
3 eggs, beaten
½ cup Italian breadcrumbs
¼ cup olive oil

Cut veal into serving pieces and trim away all membranes and grizzle. Add garlic, salt, pepper, and parsley to beaten eggs. Place cutlets with egg mixture in shallow bowl and allow to sit about 1½ hours. Dip cutlets in breadcrumbs and fry in hot oil until crisp and golden. Serve very hot.
Serves 6.

VEAL PARMESAN

Vitello Alla Parmigiana

2 pounds veal cutlets,
 ½ inch thick
Salt and pepper to taste
½ teaspoon oregano

¼ cup Parmesan cheese,
 grated
¼ cup olive oil

Trim membranes and grizzle from veal, cut into serving pieces, and pound to about ¼-inch thickness. Coat with salt, pepper, oregano, and cheese. Brown in hot oil about 5 minutes on each side. Serve very hot.
Serves 6.

Vitello Con Peperoni

1½ pounds veal cut in
  1-inch cubes
¼ cup olive oil
Salt and pepper to taste

1-pound can Italian tomatoes
4 large green peppers, sliced
1 large onion, sliced
½ cup dry white wine

Brown veal in half the oil about 15 minutes. Add salt, pepper, and tomatoes. Cover and simmer 30 minutes. Fry green peppers and onion in remaining oil until tender. Mix with veal, add wine, and simmer 15 minutes more. Serve hot. *Serves 2 to 4.*

Petto Di Agnello Al Forno

4-pound breast of lamb, cut
  into serving pieces
¼ cup lemon juice
¼ cup red wine vinegar
3 cloves garlic, chopped
1 teaspoon oregano
½ teaspoon black pepper

1 teaspoon powdered chicory
½ cup tomato paste
½ cup water
¼ teaspoon crushed red
  pepper
2 tablespoons olive oil

Place lamb in shallow baking dish and put in medium (350°F) oven for 30 minutes. Remove and drain off fat. Combine all remaining ingredients except oil and mix thoroughly. Pour over meat and sprinkle with oil; bake in 300°F oven 1 hour or until crisp. Serve very hot. *Serves 4.*

LAMB WITH ANCHOVIES

Agnello Con Acciughe

1 small leg of lamb
4 tablespoons olive oil
1 medium onion, minced
Salt and pepper to taste
1 tablespoon flour

1 cup dry white wine
1½ cups water
6 anchovy fillets, diced
1 tablespoon parsley, chopped
1 clove garlic, minced

Place meat, oil, onion, salt, and pepper in large, heavy pot. Brown meat slowly, turning occasionally. When brown, spread flour evenly over meat, add wine, and cook for 10 minutes. Add water and cover. Simmer 1½ hours or until meat is done. Stir anchovies, parsley, and garlic into gravy, and simmer for 3 minutes. Serve very hot with gravy. *Serves 4 to 6.*

ROAST LOIN OF PORK

Lombata Di Maiale Al Forno

4- to 5-pound loin of pork
2 cloves garlic, halved
Salt and pepper to taste

⅛ teaspoon marjoram
1 cup dry white wine

Have backbone loosened from ribs of roast for easier carving. Cut small slits in fatty top of roast and insert garlic halves. Sprinkle with salt, pepper, and marjoram. Place roast fat-side-up in shallow roasting pan and roast at 35 minutes per pound in 350°F oven. During last 15 minutes pour wine over roast and baste occasionally. Serve very hot. *Serves 6 to 8.*

Costolette Di Maiale Con Cavolo

1 medium onion, chopped
1 clove garlic, minced
3 tablespoons olive oil
2½ pounds pork chops,
   cut thick

1 pound cabbage, chopped
1-pound can Italian tomatoes
Salt and pepper to taste
1 cup dry white wine

Fry onion and garlic in oil until transparent. Remove them and set them aside; add chops. Brown chops on both sides, then place them with onion, garlic, cabbage, tomatoes, salt, and pepper in large pot. Simmer 30 minutes. Add wine and cook 15 minutes more or until chops are done. Serve hot. *Serves 4 to 6.*

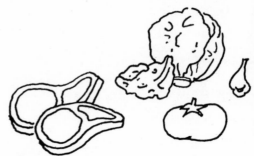

PORK CHOPS MESSINA

Costolette Di Maiale Alla Messina

1 clove garlic, sliced
3 tablespoons olive oil
6 pork chops, cut thick
¼ cup tomato paste
¼ cup water

2 large green peppers,
   cut in 1-inch pieces
1 pound fresh mushrooms,
   sliced
Salt and pepper to taste

Brown garlic in oil, then remove and discard. Brown chops slowly on both sides in oil; remove and keep hot. Add tomato paste, water, green peppers, mushrooms, chops, salt, and pep-

per. Cover and simmer 45 minutes or until chops are done. Serve very hot.
Serves 4 to 6.

CALVES' LIVER WITH ROMANO
Fegati Di Vitello Con Romano

3 tablespoons green onions, chopped
½ clove garlic, minced
1 tablespoon parsley, chopped
Salt and pepper to taste
1 pound calves' liver, sliced

4 tablespoons olive oil
2 tablespoons Italian breadcrumbs
4 tablespoons Romano cheese, grated
2 tablespoons butter, melted

Spread mixture of onions, garlic, parsley, salt, and pepper on liver slices. Brown on both sides in hot oil. Place liver in shallow baking dish and sprinkle mixed breadcrumbs and cheese over top. Dot with butter and broil until breadcrumbs are golden.
Serves 2 to 4.

BRAIN ON HOT COALS
Medualla Alla Cinnerella

1 very large onion
1 calf brain

3 or 4 large cabbage leaves

Cut onion in half. Scrape out inside of both halves, leaving a shell about ¼ inch thick. Place brain in one half of onion and cover with other half. Wrap wet cabbage leaves around entire onion; secure with toothpicks. Place in bed of hot coals 1 hour or until brain is cooked. Discard cabbage leaves and onion, and serve brain on hot platter.
Serves 2.

STUFFED BEEF HEART

Cuore Di Manzo Imbottito

1 beef heart
2 tablespoons olive oil
3 tablespoons fresh parsley,
  chopped
2 tablespoons Romano
  cheese, grated

1 clove garlic, sliced thin
Salt and pepper to taste
½ cup red raisins
1 hardboiled egg, chopped
Cooking oil
Any tomato sauce

Have beef heart cleaned and ready to stuff. Cut 1-inch slits down from center but not through bottom. Rub slits and inside with olive oil. Mix next 6 ingredients and stuff each slit with mixture. Tie string around heart so stuffing doesn't fall out. Brown on all sides in hot fat. Remove and place in tomato sauce of your choice; simmer about 1 hour. Slice cross-sectional cuts like cartwheels and place on hot platter. Serve very hot.
Serves 4 to 6.

Note: Beef tongue may be prepared in the same manner.

BROILED FRESH TRIPE

Trippa Arrostita

2 pounds fresh tripe
½ cup Italian breadcrumbs
Salt and pepper to taste
¼ cup Parmesan cheese,
  grated

¼ cup olive oil
4 tablespoons butter, melted

Wash tripe in cold water and cut into 10 squares. Boil in water to cover for 2½ hours, then drain. Mix breadcrumbs, salt, pepper, and cheese. Dip pieces of tripe in oil, then in crumb mixture. Place on greased broiler rack and broil in moderate (350°F) oven about 3 minutes on each side. Place on hot platter, dot with melted butter, and serve at once. *Serves 6 to 8.*

SAUSAGE WITH BEANS

Salsiccia Con Fagioli

*1 pound Italian sausage,
  hot or sweet
3 tablespoons olive oil
2 tablespoons tomato paste*

*Salt and pepper to taste
2 or 3 cups kidney beans,
  cooked*

Place sausage in heavy skillet and cover with water. Cook over medium heat until water evaporates, then cook 30 minutes longer, browning sausage thoroughly in its fat. Remove from pan and keep warm. Add oil to pan, then add tomato paste, salt, and pepper; cook for 10 minutes. Add sausage and simmer 20 minutes more. Place beans in serving dish and pour sausage and sauce over them. Serve very hot. *Serves 2 to 4.*

SAUSAGE WITH PEPPERS

Salsiccia Con Peperoni

*2 pounds Italian hot sausages
1 clove garlic, sliced
¼ cup olive oil
4 large green peppers,
  cut in 1-inch pieces*

*1 large onion, diced
Salt and pepper to taste
1 teaspoon parsley, chopped
¼ cup dry white wine*

Brown sausages on all sides, drain off grease, then cook slowly for 30 minutes. In separate pan fry garlic in oil until brown, then discard garlic. Add green peppers and onion to oil and fry slowly until tender; add salt, pepper, and parsley. Drain remaining grease from sausages and add sausages to peppers and onions with oil and seasonings. Add wine and simmer for another 10 minutes. Serve very hot.
Serves 4 to 6.

BAKED SAUSAGE WITH LENTILS

Salsiccia Con Lenticchie Al Forno

6 links hot Italian sausages
½ cup onion, minced
1 clove garlic, minced
¼ cup celery, minced

4 cups lentils, cooked and
* drained*
Salt and pepper to taste

Brown sausages on all sides, remove from pan, and cut into ½-inch pieces. Sauté onion, garlic, and celery in sausage drippings. Add lentils and sausages and mix thoroughly. Pour into greased casserole, sprinkle with salt and pepper, and bake in medium (350°F) oven 1 hour. Serve very hot.
Serves 2 to 4.

FRIED SQUIRREL

Scoiattolo Fritto

1 squirrel, cleaned and cut up
¼ cup red wine vinegar
½ cup flour
Salt and pepper to taste

¼ cup olive oil
1 clove garlic, halved
1 large onion, sliced

Soak squirrel in salted water 3 or 4 hours. Add vinegar and simmer slowly until almost tender. Drain and cool. Dredge squirrel in flour, salt, and pepper. Heat olive oil in large skillet. Lightly fry garlic and onion. Add squirrel and brown slowly on all sides. Serve very hot.
Serves 2 to 4.

SMOTHERED RABBIT

Coniglio Affogato

1 rabbit, 3 or 4 pounds
1/4 cup red wine vinegar
1/2 cup flour
Salt and pepper to taste
Dash of oregano
1/4 cup olive oil
2 cloves garlic, halved
6-ounce can tomato paste

6-ounce can water
1/2 teaspoon sweet basil
1/2 teaspoon parsley, chopped
1/2 green pepper, diced
1 medium onion, chopped
1/4 cup burgundy
1/2 cup mushrooms, sliced

Have rabbit cleaned and cut up. Soak in salted water about 4 hours. Add vinegar and parboil for 3 minutes. Drain water and rinse in cold water. Dredge in flour, salt, pepper, and oregano. Brown in olive oil with garlic. Add remaining ingredients and simmer 1½ hours or until tender.
Serves 4.

BROILED VENISON STEAK

Cervo Arrostito

3-pound venison steak,
   1 inch thick
2 pints dry red wine
1/4 cup olive oil

1/4 cup flour
Salt and pepper to taste
Dash of oregano

Place steaks in glass or enamel bowl and cover with wine. Marinate about 12 hours in refrigerator, turning often. Drain wine from steaks and dry with absorbent paper. Dip steaks in olive oil and flour. Broil under moderate (350°F) heat 15 minutes on each side. Brush on more oil during broiling. Sprinkle with salt, pepper, and oregano. Serve very hot. *Serves 2 to 4.*

Fowl

I know it sounds silly, but my husband used to be terrified of chickens. When he was a boy they were the only wild animals he or any of his friends saw. By "wild," he means that they were the only animals he ever saw in a cage. I'll explain.

Early every Saturday morning the chicken man used to come down the neighborhood streets hawking his wares. He had a sagging old pickup truck jammed with wooden crates full of cackling chickens, and a big, bouncing scale hanging out the back. The fascination of seeing all these caged animals in one place, bargained over by mothers, grandmothers, and aunts, was irresistible. And if any of those dangerous chickens got loose and attacked him, there were plenty of aprons to hide under.

He still recalls how awed he was by all those strong women and cackling chickens. He says he'll never forget watching his mother, who would grab one of the ferocious beasts by the legs and hold it on high, with its wings beating up a hurricane and its mouth trumpeting a horrendous cry. With a display of bravery he hasn't seen equaled since, his mother would still find the courage to beat the chicken man down a penny!

I'm sure all of this must have made quite an impression on a boy brought up in the city, but to me, a farm girl, it was the funniest thing I had ever heard. My husband isn't afraid of chickens any more, and the way he devours my Chicken Cacciatora is simply wonderful.

Ah, delicious Chicken Cacciatora. Soon after we were married, with the confidence that comes from complete ignorance, I decided to make the best Chicken Cacciatora that my husband had ever tasted. With only a vague idea of how to make it, I went to an Italian store to buy the chicken and vegetables. I meekly asked the storekeeper if I had purchased the proper ingredients, and he looked at them and said, "Eh," which I accepted as approval. Chicken Cacciatora means Hunter's Stew, because it's the way hunters cooked their birds after they had caught them. So when I got home I threw everything into the pot the way I thought hunters in the woods might have done it. I'd rather not talk about the result except to say that although my husband thought it was pretty good, he couldn't figure out what all those superfluous bones were doing in his vegetable stew. Now I know he was pulling my leg because he also reminded me that Chicken Cacciatora is a chicken stew, not a chicken *bone* stew. (He knew they were chicken bones all along.) Now, however, you can really taste the chicken in my stew.

Actually, Chicken Cacciatora isn't difficult to prepare. I think I was more impressed by its name than anything else. Had it simply been called Hunter's Stew, it might have been easier for me. If it overawes you, just compare a band of tired men tramping through the woods ravenous for anything they can find to eat, and you in a modern kitchen.

I've included a few game birds in this chapter in case you're married to one of those modern hunters who doesn't stew it in the woods but brings it home for *you* to cook.

CHICKEN HUNTER'S STYLE

Pollo Alla Cacciatora

3 tablespoons butter
4 tablespoons olive oil
2 young broilers, cut up
2 large carrots, chopped
1 cup celery, chopped
1 medium onion, chopped

Salt and pepper to taste
1/4 teaspoon oregano
1/8 teaspoon marjoram
1 tablespoon parsley, chopped
2 tablespoons tomato paste
1/2 cup dry white wine

Heat butter and oil in skillet and brown chicken on all sides. Add carrots, celery, onion, salt, pepper, oregano, marjoram, and parsley. Simmer 10 minutes or until vegetables are a little tender. Blend tomato paste and wine and add gradually. Cover and simmer 50 minutes, stirring occasionally. Serve hot.
Serves 4 to 6.

CHICKEN CASERTA

Pollo Di Caserta

2 tablespoons olive oil
1 tablespoon butter
1 clove garlic, halved
2 small fryers, cut up
Salt and pepper to taste

1/4 pound prosciutto, sliced
   thin and chopped
1/8 teaspoon marjoram
1 1/2 cups dry white wine

Heat oil and butter in heavy skillet. Add garlic; when brown, remove and discard. Rub chickens with salt and pepper and brown on all sides. Add prosciutto and marjoram. Pour wine on top. Cover and simmer until chicken is done, about 50 minutes. Serve hot with gravy from skillet.
Serves 2 to 4.

CHICKEN WITH MUSHROOMS

Pollo Con Funghi

1 large fryer, cut up
¼ cup olive oil
1 clove garlic, sliced
1 large onion, sliced
2 cups fresh mushrooms, sliced

Salt and pepper to taste
Dash of oregano
1 tablespoon parsley, chopped
½ cup dry white wine

Brown chicken in olive oil on all sides, remove to platter, and keep warm. Fry garlic until brown, then remove and discard. Add onion and mushrooms; fry lightly for 10 minutes. Add salt, pepper, oregano, and parsley; mix well. Add chicken, cover, and simmer 50 minutes. Add wine and simmer another 10 minutes. Serve very hot.
Serves 4.

CHICKEN WITH PEPPERS

Pollo Con Peperoni

1 large fryer, cut up
¼ cup olive oil
1 clove garlic, sliced
1 large onion, sliced
4 large green peppers, sliced

1-pound can Italian tomatoes
Salt and pepper to taste
Dash of oregano
1 teaspoon parsley, chopped
½ cup red or white wine

Brown chicken in hot oil on all sides, remove to platter, and keep warm. Fry garlic in oil until brown, then discard. Add onion and green peppers, and fry slowly until onions are transparent. Add tomatoes, salt, pepper, oregano, parsley, and chicken. Cover and simmer 45 minutes. Add wine and simmer another 10 minutes. Serve hot.
Serves 4.

CHICKEN WITH POTATOES AND PEPPERS

Pollo Con Patate E Peperoni

1 clove garlic, sliced	1/4 cup olive oil
1 small fryer, cut up	1 tablespoon parsley, chopped
1 large green pepper, cut in 2-inch strips	Salt and pepper to taste
	Dash of oregano
4 medium potatoes, quartered	1/8 teaspoon paprika

Put garlic slices on underside of chicken breast and at leg joints. Place chicken, green pepper, and potatoes in large, shallow baking pan, making sure they have plenty of room. Pour oil on top and sprinkle seasonings over chicken and potatoes. Put in slow (250°F to 300°F) oven for 1 hour or until chicken and potatoes are tender. Baste frequently with juice in pan. Turn heat to 375°F and brown 15 minutes more. Remove garlic and discard. Serve very hot.
Serves 2 to 4.

ROASTED CHICKEN

Pollo Arrosto

1 or 2 large fryers, whole or cut up	1 tablespoon parsley, chopped
1 clove garlic, cut in half	Salt and pepper to taste
4 tablespoons olive oil	1/4 teaspoon paprika

Rub chicken skin with garlic and set garlic aside. Place chickens in shallow baking pan. Coat with olive oil, making sure that all surfaces are covered. Sprinkle parsley, salt, pepper, and paprika over chicken. Drop garlic in bottom of pan. Roast in slow (250°F to 300°F) oven 1 hour, basting occasionally with juice and oil. Turn oven to 375°F and roast an additional 10 minutes to make chicken crisp and brown. Serve hot.

Serves 4 to 6.

CHICKEN WITH RICE

Pollo Con Riso

2 broilers or fryers, whole	*3 tablespoons butter*
Salt and pepper to taste	*1 cup rice*
1 medium carrot, quartered	*1 small onion, chopped*
2 sprigs fresh parsley	*¼ cup Parmesan cheese,*
1 stalk celery, quartered	*grated*
1 medium onion, whole	

Cover chickens with water and bring to boil quickly. Remove foam from top of water. Add salt, pepper, carrot, parsley, celery, and whole onion. Cover and simmer 1 hour or until tender. In separate pan place butter, rice, and chopped onion; brown lightly. Add chicken broth from time to time and cook until rice is tender. Add cheese and mix well. Place chicken on platter with rice around it. Pour remaining broth on top. Serve very hot.

Serves 4 to 6.

CHICKEN TETRAZZINI

Pollo Alla Tetrazzini

5-pound stewing chicken,
   cut up
Salt and pepper to taste
1 pound spaghetti
3 slices bacon, diced
½ clove garlic, minced
1 medium green pepper,
   chopped

1 medium onion, chopped
7½-ounce jar roasted red
   peppers, cut up
1 cup mushrooms, sliced and
   cooked
1 cup Romano cheese, grated

Cover chicken with water, and add salt and pepper. Simmer 2½ hours or until meat is ready to fall from bones. Remove meat from bones and dice. Cook spaghetti in chicken broth until tender, then drain; save 1 cup broth. Brown bacon in large skillet. Add garlic, green pepper, and onion, and brown lightly. Add roasted red peppers, mushrooms, and cheese; mix and heat thoroughly. Add chicken and spaghetti and simmer about 10 minutes. If too dry, moisten with a little chicken broth. Serve very hot.
Serves 6 to 8.

CHICKEN LIVERS WITH ARTICHOKES

Fegatini Di Pollo Con Carciofi

4 large artichokes
3 tablespoons lemon juice
2 tablespoons olive oil
Salt and pepper to taste
⅛ teaspoon marjoram
1 tablespoon parsley, chopped

¼ cup butter
¼ cup green onions, chopped
2 pounds chicken livers
3 slices bacon, fried and
   crumbled

75

Remove outer leaves and chokes; slice each artichoke in 6 pieces. Soak in water to cover with lemon juice for 10 minutes. Remove from water and drain. Brown artichokes in hot olive oil. Add salt, pepper, marjoram, and parsley; simmer over medium heat for 10 minutes. Melt butter in separate pan, brown onions and livers lightly, and cook for 10 minutes. Add bacon, mix well, and add to artichokes. Mix thoroughly and cook about 5 minutes. Serve very hot.
Serves 2 to 4.

DUCK WITH LENTILS

Anitra Con Lenticchie

1 medium duck, 4 to 6
  pounds, cleaned
Salt and pepper to taste
3 tablespoons olive oil
2 slices bacon, diced
½ clove garlic, minced
½ cup green onions, chopped

1 bay leaf
1 teaspoon parsley, chopped
½ cup celery, chopped
1 medium carrot, chopped
½ cup dry white wine
2 cups lentils, cooked and
  drained

Rub inside of duck with salt and pepper. Put duck in heavy, deep pot and add all remaining ingredients except wine and lentils. Brown duck slowly on all sides. Add wine and cook slowly until wine is evaporated. Add water to cover duck. Cover pot and cook over medium heat 50 minutes or until duck is tender. Remove fat from juice and pour juice over cooked lentils and duck. Serve very hot.
Serves 4.

ROASTED PHEASANT

Fagiano Arrostito

1 pheasant, 2 to 3 pounds,
   cleaned
3 tablespoons olive oil
Salt and pepper to taste
Dash of sage
Dash of marjoram
2 slices salt pork, about
   ⅛ inch thick
1 cup dry white wine

Rub pheasant inside and out with oil, salt, and pepper. Sprinkle with sage and marjoram and put salt pork slices over top. Place pheasant in shallow, greased roasting pan and roast in medium (350°F) oven 1 hour or until tender, basting occasionally. Turn oven to hot (400°F), pour wine over pheasant, and brown for 10 minutes, basting frequently. Serve very hot.
Serves 2.

SMOTHERED PIGEONS

Piccioni Affogati

4 medium-sized pigeons,
   cleaned
1 clove garlic, halved
4 tablespoons olive oil
4 tablespoons butter
½ teaspoon sage
⅛ teaspoon marjoram
Salt and pepper to taste
4 slices bacon, diced
½ cup hot water
1 tablespoon parsley, chopped
1 medium onion, sliced
1 cup mushrooms, sliced
1 lemon quarter

Rub pigeons inside and out with garlic. Brush with olive oil. Rub butter, sage, marjoram, salt, and pepper on inside. Brown bacon slowly and remove from pan. Brown pigeons on all sides quickly in bacon fat. Replace bacon. Add water, parsley, onion, mushrooms, and lemon. Cover and simmer 30 minutes or until tender. Serve hot.
Serves 4.

Vegetables

Who ever heard of fried spinach? I never had, and until you read this chapter you probably won't believe what can happen to vegetables after Italians get hold of them. You can't trust them simply to boil a vegetable, butter it, and then sprinkle it with salt and pepper — *thank goodness!* You haven't lived until you've had a dumpy little cauliflower Italian style.

There are certain things that should and should not be done to plain, down-to-earth vegetables. Take the clove of garlic, for instance. I was under the mistaken impression shared by many that to cook good Italian food you had to smother everything with garlic. *Wrong!* Some of the first dishes I produced for my husband brought tears to his eyes — not for any aesthetic reasons, but because the odor of garlic was so strong that it almost asphyxiated him. I've learned that only a whisper of garlic is necessary. Although Italians use garlic in much of their cooking, it is treated with great respect.

This chapter will bring great respect to your table, and if you have any vegetable haters around your house, these recipes are guaranteed to win them over.

BREADED ARTICHOKES

Carciofi Panati

1 cup Italian breadcrumbs
2 tablespoons Romano
  cheese, grated
Salt and pepper to taste
1 tablespoon parsley, chopped

2 eggs, beaten
6 to 8 artichoke hearts,
  parboiled
1 clove garlic, sliced
1/4 cup olive oil

Mix breadcrumbs with cheese, salt, pepper, and parsley. Put eggs in separate bowl and dip each heart first into eggs, then into crumb mixture. Fry garlic in oil until brown, then remove and discard. Fry hearts in oil until golden. Serve very hot.
Serves 2 to 4.

STUFFED ARTICHOKES

Carciofi Imbottiti

6 artichokes
2 cups Italian breadcrumbs
7-ounce can pitted black
  olives, chopped fine
2½ teaspoons salt

½ teaspoon black pepper
½ cup juice from can of
  olives
¾ cup olive oil

Cut off tops of artichokes. Peel off dead leaves and discard. Cut out center cores then cut off stems. Peel stems and chop fine. Mix breadcrumbs, olives, and artichoke stems. Add 1½ teaspoons salt, the pepper, the juice from olives, and ½ cup olive oil. Mix until moist. Open and fill center of artichokes, then spread leaves and fill with mixture. Place in 8-inch glass baking dish.

Make a basting liquid of ¼ cup olive oil, 1 cup water, and 1 teaspoon salt, and pour into bottom of baking dish around artichokes. Cover and cook on top of stove over low heat for 1 hour. Baste every 15 minutes, moving artichokes slightly to prevent sticking. If liquid dries before cooking is done, add a little more water to bottom of pan. Serve hot. *Serves 6.*

BEANS AND GREENS

Fagioli E Minestra

1 pound dried white beans (Cannellini)
½ pound pepperoni sausage

2 pounds endive or escarole
Salt to taste
Olive oil to taste
Black pepper to taste

Wash and sort beans. Put in large pot and cover with water. Cut sausage into 3 sections and add to beans. Boil for 3 minutes, then turn off heat and allow to stand for 1 hour. Turn heat on and cook slowly until beans are tender. Clean endive or escarole, put in large pot, and cover with water. Add salt and simmer until tender. Mix beans, sausage, and greens together in large bowl. Before serving, sprinkle with olive oil and pepper. Serve very hot. *Serves 6.*

BEAN CASSEROLE NEAPOLITAN

Casseruola Di Fagioli Alla Napoletana

1 pound Italian green or
  yellow flat string beans
1 medium onion, minced
1 clove garlic, minced
1/4 cup olive oil
6-ounce can tomato paste
8-ounce can tomato puree

6-ounce can cold water
1/2 teaspoon sweet basil
1/2 teaspoon oregano
Salt and pepper to taste
1/4 cup Romano cheese,
  grated

Wash beans and cut into 2-inch pieces. Boil in salted water until tender, then drain. Fry onion and garlic in oil, add tomato paste, tomato puree, and water, and blend. Add basil, oregano, salt, and pepper. Simmer uncovered until thickened, about 1 hour. Put beans in casserole and cover with sauce. Bake in moderate (350°F) oven 1/2 hour. Sprinkle with cheese and serve very hot.
Serves 2 to 4.

BROCCOLI WITH ROMANO CHEESE

Broccoli Con Romano

1 large bunch broccoli
1/4 cup olive oil
1 clove garlic, sliced
Salt and pepper to taste

1/4 cup dry white wine
1/4 cup Romano cheese,
  grated

Boil broccoli until just tender but not soft. Heat oil and fry garlic until brown, then remove and discard. Add salt, pepper, and wine to oil. Simmer 5 minutes. Pour over broccoli and sprinkle with cheese. Serve very hot.
Serves 4.

BREADED CAULIFLOWER

Cavolfiore Panato

1 large head cauliflower
1 cup breadcrumbs
2 tablespoons Romano
   cheese, grated
Salt and pepper to taste

1 tablespoon parsley, chopped
2 eggs, beaten
1 clove garlic, sliced
¼ cup olive oil

Wash cauliflower and separate into serving pieces. Parboil until just tender, then drain and cool. Mix breadcrumbs with cheese, salt, pepper, and parsley. Put eggs in separate bowl and dip each piece of cauliflower first into eggs, then into crumb mixture. Fry garlic in oil until brown, then remove and discard. Fry cauliflower in oil until crisp and golden. Serve at once.
Serves 2 to 4.

BAKED STUFFED EGGPLANT

Melanzana Imbottita Al Forno

2 eggplants, cut in half
   lengthwise
2 cups mushrooms, cooked
   and chopped
¼ cup black olives, chopped
1 small onion, minced
1 cup Italian tomatoes,
   drained

1 cup Italian breadcrumbs
1 teaspoon salt
¼ cup Romano cheese,
   grated
½ cup water

Cut inside pulp from eggplants; shells should be about ¼ inch thick. Mix pulp with mushrooms, olives, onion, tomatoes, breadcrumbs, and salt. Fill shells with mixture and

sprinkle cheese over the top. Place stuffed eggplant in greased baking dish with water. Bake in moderate (350°F) oven 45 minutes or until shells are tender. Serve hot.
Serves 4.

SICILIAN EGGPLANT

Melanzana Alla Siciliana

1-pound-can Italian tomatoes, strained
3 tablespoons tomato paste
½ cup olive oil
1 large eggplant
Salt and pepper to taste
1 cup breadcrumbs

½ cup Pecorino cheese, grated
1 tablespoon parsley, chopped
2 cloves garlic, sliced thin
¼ pound Mozzarella cheese, sliced thin

Mix tomatoes, tomato paste, and 3 tablespoons oil and simmer in a skillet for 20 minutes. Wash eggplant and slice into ½-inch slices. Place slices in bowl of hot water for 10 minutes. Drain and dry with towel. Fry eggplant in remaining oil until golden brown, add salt and pepper, and remove from pan. Mix breadcrumbs, Pecorino cheese, parsley, and garlic. Put a layer of eggplant in baking pan, sprinkle with breadcrumb mixture, and add a layer of tomato sauce. Re-

peat until all ingredients are used. Place Mozzarella slices over the top and bake in moderate (350°F) oven for 15 minutes. Serve very hot.
Serves 4.

FRIED ESCAROLE

Escarola Fritta

½ cup olive oil
2 cloves garlic, sliced
1 tablespoon Romano cheese, grated

1 pound escarole, cleaned and cut in half
Salt and pepper to taste

Heat oil in large skillet and brown garlic slowly. Add cheese, escarole, salt, and pepper. Mix and cook for 20 minutes or until tender. Serve very hot.
Serves 4.

LENTILS WITH OIL

Lenticchie Con Olio

1 pound dried lentils
2-inch cube salt pork
1 clove garlic, halved
1 medium onion, minced

Salt and pepper to taste
Olive oil to taste
Freshly grated Romano or Pecorino cheese to taste

Wash and sort lentils. Put in large pot and cover with salted water. Add salt pork, garlic, and onion and bring to boil. Turn heat down and simmer slowly until tender, 45 minutes to 1 hour. Sprinkle with salt, pepper, oil, and cheese. Serve very hot.
Serves 6 to 8.

MUSHROOMS WITH ONIONS
Funghi Con Cipolla

1/4 cup olive oil
1 pound mushrooms, sliced
1 large sweet onion, sliced

Salt and pepper to taste
1/4 cup dry white wine

Heat oil in heavy skillet and add mushrooms, onion, salt, and pepper. Cook over high heat 5 minutes, stirring to prevent burning. Lower heat and add wine. Cover and simmer 35 minutes or until mushrooms are tender. Serve very hot.
Serves 2 to 4.

STUFFED MUSHROOM CAPS
Funghi Imbottiti

12 large mushrooms
1 cup soaked Italian bread
   (squeeze out water)
2 links fried Italian sausage,
   broken up
1 egg, beaten
1/4 cup Romano or Parmesan
   cheese, grated

1/4 teaspoon oregano
1 sprig parsley, chopped
Salt and pepper to taste
1/4 cup olive oil
1 clove garlic, sliced
2 cups Sicilian Sauce
   (page 35)

Parboil mushrooms in salted water for 5 minutes, then drain. Combine bread, mushroom stems, sausage, and egg; mix well. Add cheese, oregano, parsley, salt, and pepper. Fill mushroom caps with mixture, then sauté in oil with garlic, stuffing-side-down, until brown; do not turn. Oil must be very hot so stuffing won't stick. Put Sicilian Sauce in baking casserole, gently lift mushrooms from oil, and place on top of sauce. Cover and bake in moderate (350°F) oven for 30 minutes,

then uncover until domes are light brown. Serve in casserole or on bed of rice or noodles.
Serves 4 to 6.

VARIATION
Omit Sicilian Sauce; add onion and green pepper rings to oil and fry with mushrooms until tender.

PEOPLE'S PEAS
Piselli Del Popolo

½ cup olive oil
1 clove garlic, chopped
1 medium onion, diced
1 tablespoon Romano cheese, grated

1-pound-can green peas, drained
Salt and pepper to taste

Heat oil in heavy skillet and fry garlic and onion slowly for 10 minutes. Add cheese, peas, salt, and pepper. Mix and simmer for 5 minutes. Serve hot.
Makes about 2 cups.

GREEN PEPPERS WITH ONION
Peperoni Con Cipolla

6 large green peppers
¼ cup olive oil
1 clove garlic, minced

3 large onions, sliced
Salt and pepper to taste
Dash of oregano

Wash green peppers and remove stems and seeds. Cut lengthwise in 1-inch strips. Heat oil in skillet and add garlic, onions,

and green peppers. Coat thoroughly with oil and fry over hot flame for 5 minutes. Stir to prevent burning. When light brown, lower flame. Add salt, pepper, and oregano. Cover and simmer until tender. Serve hot.
Serves 4 to 6.

FRIED SPINACH

Spinaci Fritti

½ cup olive oil
3 cloves garlic, whole
1 tablespoon Romano cheese, grated

1 pound spinach, cleaned
Salt and pepper to taste

Heat oil in skillet and brown garlic slowly for 10 minutes. Add cheese, spinach, salt, and pepper. Mix and simmer for 20 minutes or until spinach is tender. Serve hot.
Serves 4.

FRIED SQUASH

Cucuzza Fritta

2 eggs, beaten
Dash of oregano
Salt and pepper to taste
4 tablespoons Romano cheese, grated

½ cup breadcrumbs
1 pound squash, cleaned and cut in ½-inch slices
½ cup olive oil

Mix eggs with oregano, salt, and pepper. Mix cheese and breadcrumbs together. Dip squash first into eggs, then into breadcrumbs. Fry in oil until crisp and golden. Serve very hot.
Serves 4 to 6.

Zucchini Al Forno

1 medium onion, chopped
1 clove garlic, chopped
2 tablespoons olive oil
1 pound zucchini, sliced thin

1 cup Italian tomatoes,
  drained
¼ teaspoon salt
¼ cup Pecorino cheese,
  grated

Sauté onion and garlic in oil for 5 minutes. Add zucchini and cook over low flame, stirring, for 5 minutes more. Add tomatoes and salt. Cover and simmer for 10 minutes, then pour into small greased casserole. Sprinkle cheese on top and bake in moderate (350°F) oven for 20 minutes or until cheese is bubbling. Serve very hot.
Serves 4.

Salads

I think it's nice to have a husband who will toss a salad for you. I was lucky, because my husband enjoys making salads and they are always delicious. I must admit that the first time I saw him liberally sprinkling a beautiful salad with grated Italian cheese I was aghast, but it tasted so good I no longer eat salad without it. To my husband, salad greens mean *salad greens,* including escarole, endive, romaine, and spinach; if someone puts a salad of iceberg lettuce in front of him, he looks as though he had been mortally wounded.

Italian people are also very fond of fresh dandelion greens.

You can see them early in the morning while the dew is still on the ground, picking only the tenderest shoots for their dinner.

With salads, the most appealing one is the simplest — just a bowl of greens with oil and salt. There aren't any basic rules for making salads other than using fresh ingredients and, usually, olive oil. But the number of different salads that can be made is endless; the following recipes will show you some of the things that can be done with vegetables and greens.

ANCHOVY AND CHEESE SALAD

Insalata D'Acciughe E Provolone

1 head romaine, cleaned
2-ounce can anchovy fillets, halved
¼ pound Provolone cheese, cut in strips
¼ cup olive oil

4 tablespoons red wine vinegar
1 clove garlic, sliced
Salt and pepper to taste
Dash of oregano

Break romaine in bite-sized pieces in large salad bowl. Add anchovies and cheese strips. Combine oil, vinegar, garlic, salt, pepper, and oregano. Pour over salad and mix well. Serve at once.
Serves 2 to 4.

ITALIAN CELERY SALAD

Insalata Di Finocchio

5 stalks Italian celery, cleaned
¼ cup olive oil

Dash of oregano
Salt and pepper to taste

Slice Italian celery in 1-inch pieces; add oil, oregano, salt, and pepper. Mix well and serve.
Serves 2 to 4.

CHICK PEA SALAD

Insalata Di Ceci

½ cup olive oil
3 tablespoons red wine
  vinegar
1 teaspoon oregano
2 tablespoons parsley,
  chopped

Salt and pepper to taste
1 large red onion, slivered
1 clove garlic, mashed
½ cup pimientos, slivered
4 cups chick peas, cooked

Blend first 5 ingredients. Add onion, garlic, and pimientos; mix well. Pour in deep bowl and add chick peas. Chill about 1 hour.
Serves 2 to 4.

DANDELION SALAD

Insalata Di Cicoria Fina

1 pound dandelions, cleaned
1 small red onion, chopped
1 hardboiled egg, chopped
1 clove garlic, sliced
4 tablespoons olive oil

3 tablespoons red wine
  vinegar
Salt and pepper to taste
2 tablespoons Romano
  cheese, grated

Break dandelions into bite-sized pieces in salad bowl. Add onion, hardboiled egg, and garlic. Blend oil, vinegar, salt,

and pepper. Pour over dandelions, mix well, and sprinkle with grated cheese.
Serves 2 to 4.

Insalata Di Fagioli Rossi

½ cup olive oil
4 tablespoons red wine
  vinegar
1 tablespoon parsley, chopped
Salt and pepper to taste

4 cups red kidney beans,
  cooked
1 stalk Italian celery, cut in
  1-inch pieces
½ cup green onions, chopped

Combine oil, vinegar, parsley, salt, and pepper. Place beans, Italian celery, and onions in deep bowl and coat with marinade; mix. Cover and chill about 1 hour.
Serves 2 to 4.

Insalata Mista

½ head escarole, cleaned
½ head romaine, cleaned
½ pound tender spinach
  leaves, cleaned
½ cup olive oil
Juice from 1 lemon

1 tablespoon parsley, chopped
Salt and pepper to taste
Dash of crushed red peppers
1 medium onion, sliced
1 clove garlic, sliced
½ cup ripe olives, sliced

Break greens into bite-sized pieces and put in large salad bowl. Mix oil, lemon juice, parsley, salt, pepper, and red

peppers. Add onion, garlic, and olives. Pour dressing over salad and mix well. Serve at once.
Serves 4 to 6.

ORANGE AND OLIVE SALAD

Insalata D'Arancia E Olive

2 large oranges, peeled
4 tablespoons dry white wine
¼ cup olive oil
1 small green onion, minced

Salt and pepper to taste
Dash of oregano
1 cup pitted black olives

Slice oranges in ¼-inch slices, and place in large bowl. Mix wine, oil, onion, salt, pepper, and oregano. Pour over oranges, add olives, and mix gently. Chill about 20 minutes and serve.
Serves 2 to 4.

STRING BEAN SALAD

Insalata Di Fagiolini

½ cup olive oil
3 tablespoons red wine
  vinegar
1 clove garlic, sliced thin
1 very small onion, minced
1 tablespoon parsley, chopped
Salt and pepper to taste

2 cups green or yellow string
  beans, cooked
1 stalk Italian celery, cut in
  1-inch pieces
1 tablespoon pimiento,
  minced

Combine oil and vinegar, and add garlic, onion, parsley, salt, and pepper. Pour over string beans, Italian celery, and pimiento. Cover and chill about 1 hour.
Serves 2 to 4.

TOMATO SALAD

Insalata Di Pomodoro

4 large, ripe tomatoes,
 quartered
¼ cup olive oil
2 cloves garlic, sliced thin

Salt and pepper to taste
Dash of oregano
1 tablespoon parsley, chopped

Place tomatoes in large bowl and add remaining ingredients.
Stir gently to coat tomatoes thoroughly. Cover and chill about
1 hour. Stir again and serve.
Serves 2 to 4.

TOMATO SALAD WITH TUNA FISH

Insalata Di Pomodoro E Tonno

4 large, ripe tomatoes,
 quartered
7-ounce-can white chunk
 tuna
1 medium onion, sliced
1 clove garlic, sliced
¼ cup olive oil

1 tablespoon parsley, chopped
Juice from 1 lemon or
 3 tablespoons red wine
 vinegar
Dash of oregano
Salt and pepper to taste

Place tomatoes with tuna fish in deep bowl. Add onion and
garlic and stir gently, breaking tuna fish into bite-sized
pieces. Blend oil, parsley, lemon juice or vinegar, and seasonings and pour over tomatoes and fish. Chill about 1 hour.
Stir again gently and serve.
Serves 2 to 4.

Desserts

If I had trouble with tomato sauce, I was absolutely terrified at the idea of making Italian desserts. All those layers of cake and custard and those smug little cookies. I forgot about them for a while, preferring to concentrate on the body of the meals. As a matter of fact, I tried to ignore them completely.

I was very relieved to discover that my husband didn't eat rich, heavy desserts. A bowl of fresh fruit, some cheese, nuts, or a little fruit cordial are his favorites to put the topper on a wonderful meal. Of course, there are holidays, birthdays, and all sorts of special occasions and, true to form, there were hun-

97

dreds of recipes and instructions about how to make desserts for these events. I've included some of the family favorites in this chapter, especially the ones I enjoy making.

One nice thing about an Italian meal is that if the main course demanded all your energy and you've none left for dessert, there's always the simple and elegant standby, peaches and wine.

SWEET CHEESE PUDDING

Budino Dolce Di Ricotta

1 tablespoon orange rind, *4 tablespoons milk*
  grated *1 teaspoon vanilla*
½ cup chocolate chips *1 pound Ricotta cheese*

Combine all ingredients, mix thoroughly, and chill; serve in pudding dishes. Can be topped with slivered almonds.
Serves 6 to 8.

WINE CUSTARD

Zabaglione

4 tablespoons powdered *6 eggs, whole*
  sugar *6 tablespoons Marsala*
Dash of salt

Combine sugar, salt, and eggs in double boiler over hot water. Beat constantly for 10 minutes. Add Marsala little by little, beating constantly. Do not allow to boil. When stiff, pour into parfait glasses and chill.
Serves 6.

APRICOT COOKIES

Pasticcini Di Albicocca

1/2 cup butter	1/4 cup milk
1/2 cup granulated sugar	1 1/2 cups apricot preserves
2 whole eggs	1 egg yolk
1 teaspoon vanilla	1 tablespoon water
3 cups sifted flour	1 cup blanched almonds,
1 teaspoon baking powder	slivered
1/4 teaspoon salt	Colored candies

Cream butter and add sugar, whole eggs, and vanilla. Beat until well blended and light. Add dry ingredients and milk, mixing well. Chill overnight. Roll thin on floured board and cut in 2-inch squares. Put 1 teaspoon preserves on center of each square. Roll up and brush with egg yolk mixed with water. Sprinkle with almonds and candies. Bake in medium (350°F) oven for 10 minutes.
Makes about 4 dozen cookies.

CHEESE COOKIES

Pasticcini Di Ricotta

1/2 pound butter	1/2 pound walnut meats
1/2 pound Ricotta cheese	Granulated sugar to taste
2 cups flour	Light cream to taste
Powdered sugar	

Cream butter and cheese, then gradually mix in flour. Shape into ball. Chill in refrigerator 3 hours. Roll out into powdered sugar and cut into thin strips. Make filling by combining nuts, granulated sugar, and enough cream to hold mixture

99

together. Put filling in dough strips and roll up. Bake in medium (350°F) oven 10 or 12 minutes.
Makes about 2 dozen cookies.

MACAROONS

Amaretti

½ pound almonds, blanched | 2 egg whites
1 cup granulated sugar | ½ teaspoon almond extract

Chop almonds, then pound to a powder. Add sugar and mix. Beat egg whites until very stiff and add to almonds and sugar. Add almond extract and blend well. Shape into balls about 2 inches in diameter. Place on greased cookie sheet about 1 inch apart. Bake in medium (350°F) oven 5 minutes or until golden brown.
Makes about 1 dozen macaroons.

SPONGE CAKE

Pane Di Spagna

1 cup sifted flour | 1½ teaspoons almond extract
¼ teaspoon salt | 5 eggs, separated
2 teaspoons lemon rind, | 1 cup granulated sugar
grated

Sift flour and salt together several times. Add lemon rind and almond extract to beaten egg yolks; beat until very thick. Beat egg whites until stiff, and gradually fold in sugar. Fold in egg yolks. Gradually sift flour over top and fold in. Bake in ungreased 10-inch cake pan in medium (350°F) oven 1

hour. Turn pan upside down on rack for 1 hour. Remove pan.
Makes 1 10-inch cake.

ITALIAN RUM CAKE

Zuppa Inglese

1 sponge cake, 10 inches in
   diameter
1 cup sweet rum
1 recipe Zabaglione (Wine
   Custard) (page 98)

1 ounce crème de cacao
½ cup glazed fruit, minced
¼ cup almonds, finely
   chopped

Cut sponge cake into 3 layers. Place 1 layer on cake dish. Pour half of rum over it. Spread with third of Zabaglione. Place second layer of cake over this and pour crème de cacao on top. Spread with another third of Zabaglione. Place third layer of cake over this and pour remaining rum on top. Spread remaining Zabaglione over top and sides, then sprinkle with glazed fruit and chopped almonds. Chill in refrigerator before serving.
Serves 10 to 12.

HELEN'S CHERRY CAKE

Pasticcino Di Ciliègia Alla Elena

1 cup shortening
2 cups granulated sugar
4 eggs, separated
1 cup Maraschino cherries,
   chopped, with juice
1 cup milk

3½ cups flour
4 tablespoons baking powder
¼ teaspoon salt
¼ cup almonds, chopped
1 teaspoon vanilla extract
1 teaspoon lemon extract

Cream shortening, add 1 cup sugar, and cream them together. Add beaten egg yolks and mix until smooth. Alternately add cherry juice and milk, little by little. Sift flour, baking powder, and salt together, add to mixture, and blend until smooth. Add cherries, nuts, and flavorings. Make meringue of egg whites and remaining cup of sugar; fold into batter. Bake in three 8-inch cake pans in medium (350°F) oven for 30 minutes.

Makes three 8-inch layers.

PEACHES AND WINE

Pesche E Vino

1 or 2 peaches, peeled and
  sliced

2 or 3 ounces burgundy

Chill peaches and wine. Place peaches in large parfait glass, cover with wine, and serve.
Serves 1.

Beverages

When we were first married, my husband bought me a four-cup Italian coffeepot. It's called a macchinetta. As a bachelor he had a little two-cup one that he used quite often. We bought ours in the Italian food store along with that wonderful dark Italian coffee. This is another area where the process is taken quite seriously, but actually this coffee is very easy to make.

My husband prefers his espresso with a teaspoon of Fernet Branca in it. (Fernet Branca is an Italian appetite stimulant that has a taste like peppermint and is sold in all Italian food stores.) This simple ritual is a lot of fun. It seems that no sooner has the little pot been put over the flame than it gives off its little hiss, which heralds its readiness to be enjoyed. Espresso is a delightful demitasse that takes away the "full" feeling. These Italians have thought of everything.

In this chapter I'll just set down two espresso recipes, because once you have the pot and the Italian roasted coffee, there's not much to do except enjoy it.

I won't go into a wine list as most conventional cookbooks do, because my husband won't let me. He feels that wine is a very personal pleasure and that wine protocol notwithstanding, you should drink the kind you like best regardless of the type of food being served. He says that all wine lists should be torn up and fed to sommeliers. Ah, that beautiful independence. I'm sure that if more people took this relaxed attitude they would find drinking wine a lot more enjoyable. With my wine list taken away from me, all I can say is, *"Salute!"*

ITALIAN COFFEE

Caffè Espresso

4 coffee measures (8 level tablespoons) dark Italian-roast pulverized coffee
1½ cups water

Put macchinetta over heat and wait for small opening in bottom to steam. Remove from heat and turn upside down until all brew has dripped through. Serve in demitasse cups with a twist of lemon, ½ teaspoon Fernet Branca, sugar, or a little liqueur. Never add cream.
Serves 4.

Caffè Cappuccino

Make Italian Coffee (see previous recipe). Combine steaming coffee with equal quantities of steaming milk. Pour into tall demitasse cups and sprinkle with cinnamon or nutmeg. This is sometimes served with whipped cream and a touch of grated orange peel.
Serves 4.

My father has always kept a dozen or so chickens around his farm. He loves chickens. Even more than the chickens, he loves eggs. My father's chickens live in an insulated coop that has louvered air ducts and handmade feed boxes. The chickens get all of the best green scraps from his kitchen; in the winter they get them cooked. He coddles them, talks to them, and sits by their side when they're sick. All of this is for one purpose — so that the family can have a decent, fresh egg.

We never had "supermarket" eggs in our house. My father is sure that poultry ranches don't have the time to treat chickens individually and that when the eggs are laid, they are stored for months and months. From his viewpoint, an egg is only good if it is one day old and if, when it's broken, the yolk stands up two feet high and screams, *"I'm fresh!"*

My father uses a very complicated system for storing eggs in the refrigerator which drives my mother mad. Each egg is marked on top with the initial of the day of the week it was laid. Sometimes he has trouble with Tuesday and Thursday or Saturday and Sunday, and my poor mother never knows which ones to use first. Any egg older than one week is hardboiled or given away. Daddy thinks that eggs should be softboiled or poached gently with butter. Once in a while you can fry some, but eggs are a chicken's gift and should be treated with respect.

The reason I go into all of this is that Daddy doesn't know what Italians do with eggs. I haven't dared to tell him. It would make him tremble to think about eggs with anchovies or eggs with hot peppers. I know that eggs with pepperoni sausage, not to mention the "Farmer's Eggs" in this chapter, would move him to tears. I hope my father skips this chapter; it will only hurt him.

On the other hand, my husband shudders when he sees Daddy boiling the life out of beautiful, fresh mushrooms. Someday I may get Daddy to try an Italian egg dish, but I know for certain that my husband will never eat my father's boiled mushrooms.

EGGS WITH ANCHOVIES

Uova Con Acciughe

6 or 7 anchovy fillets	*4 tablespoons butter*
1 teaspoon onion, minced	*6 eggs, beaten*
2 sprigs parsley, chopped	*Black pepper to taste*

Mash anchovy fillets, onion, and parsley to form a paste. Heat butter in skillet and add eggs and pepper, stirring constantly. When eggs are almost done, add anchovy mixture and mix well. Serve hot.

Serves 4 to 6.

EGGS WITH BEEF

Uova Con Manzo

3 tablespoons olive oil	1 teaspoon parsley, chopped
1 clove garlic, sliced	Salt and pepper to taste
1 medium onion, minced	6 eggs, beaten
1/2 pound ground lean beef	1/4 cup Parmesan cheese,
1 medium tomato, diced	grated

Heat oil in heavy skillet and brown garlic, then remove and discard. Fry onion gently in oil until transparent. Add meat, tomato, parsley, salt, and pepper. Mix and fry slowly for 15 minutes. Add eggs; stir constantly until eggs are done. Sprinkle with grated cheese and serve hot.

Serves 4 to 6.

EGGS WITH CHICKEN LIVERS

Uova Con Fegatini Di Pollo

2 tablespoons olive oil	6 eggs
2 tablespoons butter	1 1/2 cups light cream
1 small onion, minced	1/4 cup Parmesan cheese,
1 pound chicken livers	grated
Salt and pepper to taste	1 teaspoon pimiento, minced

Heat oil and butter and sauté onion until tender. Add chicken livers, salt, and pepper, and brown lightly. Pour into greased casserole. Drop eggs one by one on top of livers. Add cream and sprinkle with cheese and pimiento. Bake in medium (350°F) oven for 15 minutes. Serve hot.
Serves 4 to 6.

FARMER'S EGGS

Uova Alla Agricoltora

2 medium onions, minced
1/4 cup olive oil
2 cups green peas, cooked
3 eggs, beaten

1/2 cup Pecorino or Romano
  cheese, grated
Salt and pepper to taste

Fry onions in oil until golden, add peas, and stir. Add eggs, cheese, salt, and pepper. Mix and cook until eggs are set. Serve hot.
Serves 2.

EGGS WITH MACARONI

Uova Con Pasta

3 tablespoons olive oil
6 eggs, beaten
Salt and pepper to taste
1/2 cup Ditalini, cooked and
  drained

3/4 cup Plain Tomato Sauce
  (page 34) or any leftover
  tomato sauce
1/4 cup Romano cheese,
  grated
Crushed hot red peppers
  (optional)

Heat oil and add eggs, salt, and pepper. Cook slowly, stirring

constantly, until eggs are set. Reduce heat; add Ditalini and tomato sauce. Mix well and serve with cheese and red peppers.
Serves 4 to 6.

EGGS WITH PEPPERS

Uova Con Peperoni

4 tablespoons olive oil
1 clove garlic, sliced
1 small onion, minced

4 large green peppers, cut in
  1/2-inch strips
6 eggs
Salt and pepper to taste

Heat oil in heavy skillet and fry garlic until golden brown, then remove and discard. Fry onion gently in oil for 5 minutes. Add green peppers and fry slowly until almost soft. Then add eggs one by one, stirring constantly until done. Add salt and pepper. Serve very hot.
Serves 2 to 4.

EGGS WITH PEPPERONI SAUSAGE

Uova Con Pepperoni

3 tablespoons olive oil
1 small onion, minced
6-inch length pepperoni
  sausage, sliced

6 eggs, beaten
Salt to taste

Heat oil in heavy skillet. Fry onion slowly until golden. Add sausage and fry 5 minutes. Add eggs and salt; stir constantly until eggs are done. Serve hot.
Serves 4 to 6.

HOT DRY PEPPERS WITH EGGS

Pepe Forte Con Uova

2 hot, dried cherry peppers   6 eggs
1/4 cup olive oil   Salt to taste

Break peppers into pieces and fry slowly over low heat in olive oil for 15 minutes. Break eggs into oil and peppers, add salt, and fry gently, turning over once. Serve very hot.
Serves 2 to 4.

Variation
Omit eggs and pour mixture over baked potatoes.

EGGS WITH RICE

Uova Con Riso

4 cups rice, cooked   1 cup green peas, cooked
1/3 cup butter, melted   6 eggs
1 1/2 teaspoons salt   1 or 2 sprigs fresh parsley,
1/8 teaspoon pepper   minced
1/2 cup Romano cheese,
  grated

Combine all ingredients except eggs and parsley. Spread in greased casserole, make 6 depressions in rice mixture, and drop egg in each. Sprinkle with parsley and broil 6 minutes or until eggs are set. Serve very hot.
Serves 4 to 6.

Snacks and Tidbits

The first time my husband took me to his mother's house there were four large pots cooking on the stove. I didn't know what was in them, but there was such a variety of wonderful aromas that I thought she was preparing a feast. She wasn't; it was just her normal, everyday cooking.

I've never been in her home when there weren't at least two big pots simmering away, night or day. I didn't know then what happened to all of that food, but I do now. Every bit of it is eaten. I used to wonder if Italian women ever left the kitchen to go to bed at night. They were always cooking something, and there were always dishes being done to the constant rhythm of splashing, steaming water. They lived in the kitchen, but they enjoyed it. My mother's kitchen was like that too, but only on holidays, not every day in the year. That's part of the appeal of my husband's family. Every day is like a holiday, and there are usually plenty of people around to eat. The Italian household seems to be a round robin of meals, half-meals, and snacks. Good company is the only reason needed to start eating.

I remember a day when my husband and I visited a friend at 2 o'clock in the afternoon, which as you know is after lunch and before dinner. Well, I was given a glass of wine, a chicken leg that had been cooked in some marvelous wine sauce, a dish of beans in oil, a piece of pizza, some spring onions, a large chunk of crisp bread, a dish of marinated olives, and a hot sausage. I never did eat dinner that night. This type of "snacking" goes on all day, all year round.

About the most famous snack of all is pizza; however, the way Italians eat pizza was a surprise. I was used to seeing it topped with everything imaginable, but my husband told me that the pizzas he ate were topped only with tomato sauce. The dough was about 1/2 inch thick and the sauce was simply poured on the top before putting it into the oven, making a wonderful, tomatoey delight. Italians seldom put anything else on their "true pizza." I've given the recipe for the basic dough and added a list of toppings, in case you're used to "pizza with everything." But do try it the old-fashioned way just once. I think you'll be surprised too.

I've included antipasto in this chapter because my husband's family uses it as a snack as well as an appetizer. Sometimes it includes a great many ingredients and is eaten as a whole meal. As with pizza, only your imagination is necessary to create one.

So go ahead—jump out of bed and get that midnight snack.

Antipasto Alla Famiglia

1 head Italian celery
8 or 10 romaine leaves
½ cup pickled beets
¼ pound salami, sliced
    wafer thin
½ cup black olives
¼ pound prosciutto, sliced
    thin

½ cup peperoncini
2 hardboiled eggs, quartered
3 slices Provalone cheese
2 or 3 pimientos, sliced
Olive oil to taste
Red wine vinegar to taste
Salt and pepper to taste

Arrange Italian celery and romaine in bite-sized pieces on large cold platter. Add next 8 ingredients, arranging attractively. Before serving, sprinkle with olive oil, vinegar, salt, and pepper.
Serves 4 to 6.

Antipasto Verde

6 escarole leaves
6 romaine leaves
6 endive leaves
½ cup green olives
½ cup peperoncini
4 artichoke hearts, cooked

2 stalks celery, cut in 3-inch
    pieces
1 cucumber, sliced
½ cup black olives
Olive oil to taste
Red wine vinegar to taste
Salt and pepper to taste

Arrange escarole, romaine, and endive in bite-sized pieces on platter. Add next 6 ingredients, arranging attractively. Before serving, sprinkle with oil, vinegar, salt, and pepper.
Serves 2 to 4.

Antipasto Di Mezzanotte

½ pound fresh, garden
lettuce leaves
6 escarole leaves
¼ pound capocollo, sliced
thin
1 ripe tomato, quartered
¼ cup ripe olives
4 thin slices Mozzarella
cheese

4 roasted peppers, sliced
4 pieces cauliflower,
uncooked
4 fresh mushrooms, sliced
Olive oil to taste
Red wine vinegar to taste
Salt and pepper to taste

Arrange lettuce and escarole in bite-sized pieces on platter.
Add next 7 ingredients, arranging attractively. Sprinkle with
oil, vinegar, salt, and pepper and serve.
Serves 2 to 4.

Pane Fritto

4 slices Italian bread
4 tablespoons olive oil
Black pepper to taste
¼ pound Mozzarella cheese,
sliced thin

2-ounce-can anchovy fillets
¼ cup Romano cheese,
grated
Dash of oregano

Place bread with oil in heavy skillet and sprinkle with pepper. Place Mozzarella and anchovy fillets on each slice of
bread. Sprinkle with Romano and oregano. Brown bread
slowly until golden and thoroughly heated.
Serves 4.

COLD BEANS
Fagioli Freddi

2 cups red or white kidney
  beans, boiled and chilled
3 tablespoons olive oil
1 tablespoon red wine
  vinegar

2 tablespoons green onion,
  chopped
Salt and pepper to taste

Mix all ingredients, chill, and serve.
Serves 2 to 4.

CANTALOUPE WITH ITALIAN HAM
Melone Con Prosciutto

1 medium cantaloupe, chilled

1/4 pound prosciutto, sliced
  wafer thin

Cut melon into eighths and remove pulp. Cover each wedge
with slices of prosciutto and serve.
Serves 6 to 8.

AUNT IDA'S EASTER PIE
Pasticcio Di Pasqua Alla Zia Ida

DOUGH
4 cups flour, sifted
2 eggs
1/4 cup vegetable oil,
  plus 1 tablespoon

1/4 teaspoon salt
Pepper to taste
1/4 cup milk (enough to
  moisten)

Beat all ingredients together except milk. Gradually add just enough milk to moisten dough for kneading. Knead about 15 minutes, then allow to stand 30 minutes. Divide dough in two pieces. Roll out half on floured board to fit bottom and sides of greased 13x9x2 baking pan. Set aside other half to cover filling.

FILLING

15 eggs, beaten
4 hardboiled eggs, diced
1 pound Italian salami, diced
1 pound fresh Mozzarella
  cheese, diced

1 cup Parmesan cheese,
  grated
Pepper to taste
1 egg, beaten

Beat eggs and add the diced Mozzarella cheese; fold in other ingredients except for the 1 beaten egg, and stir gently but firmly. Pour filling on top of dough. Roll out second piece of dough and cover filling. Tuck dough in all around and pinch ends so filling cannot come out. Brush with beaten egg and cut tiny slits in dough. Bake in moderate (375°F) oven 1½ hours. Allow to cool, then slice and serve. This pie may be stored in refrigerator, sliced, and eaten cold.
Serves 12 to 14.

SKEWERED LAMB

Spiedi Di Agnello

2 cloves garlic, chopped
Salt and pepper to taste
1 tablespoon fresh parsley,
  chopped
1 teaspoon oregano

1 leg of lamb, about 5 pounds
1 cup water
½ cup olive oil
⅓ cup red wine vinegar
1 loaf fresh Italian bread,
  sliced

Mash garlic, salt, pepper, parsley, and oregano together until

thoroughly blended. Strip meat from leg of lamb and cut into 1-inch cubes. In large glass container blend water, oil, and vinegar; add garlic mixture and lamb. Mix well, cover tightly, and marinate in refrigerator at least 24 hours. Place cubes of meat on long, metal skewers (spiedi), 6 to 8 pieces per skewer. Broil over charcoal grill until done, about 30 minutes, turning and basting frequently with marinade. With slice of bread in one hand and skewer in the other, slide meat onto bread and eat.
Serves 6 to 8.

HOT MEATBALL SANDWICH

Panino Imbottito Di Polpette

12 leftover meatballs, sliced   1 loaf fresh Italian bread
1½ cups leftover tomato
    sauce

Heat meatballs thoroughly in sauce for about 15 minutes. Place meatballs on bread and cover with sauce; cover with another slice of bread or leave open-faced. Serve immediately.
Serves 6 to 8.

MEAT LOAF SNACK

Spuntino Di Polpettone

6 slices fresh Italian bread   2 tablespoons olive oil
6 slices leftover meat loaf,   Salt and pepper to taste
    ½ inch thick   Dash of hot, crushed red
6 slices Mozzarella cheese,   peppers
    sliced wafer thin   Dash of oregano

Place bread on cookie sheet and put one slice of meat loaf on each piece of bread. Spread slices of Mozzarella over meat loaf. Combine oil, salt, pepper, red peppers, and oregano. Sprinkle on top of cheese and bake in medium (350°F) oven 15 minutes or until meat loaf is thoroughly heated and cheese is bubbling.
Serves 6.

NONNI'S ORANGE RIND SNACK

Spuntino Di Buccia D'Arancia Alla Nonni

Rinds from 3 large oranges
1/4 cup olive oil
1 teaspoon oregano
Salt and pepper to taste

3 cloves garlic, halved
1 cup red wine vinegar
1 cup ripe olives

Cut orange rinds in 1-inch pieces, place in small saucepan, and cover with water. Boil 3 minutes, then drain. Gently squeeze water from rinds. Combine remaining ingredients and add mixture to rinds. Put in glass jar with cover. Push rinds and olives to bottom of jar; do this once a day. Cover and marinate about 1 week in refrigerator. Serve cold with fresh Italian bread.
Makes 1½ to 2 cups.

PIZZA

Pizza

BASIC PIZZA

4½ cups sifted flour
2 tablespoons vegetable oil
1 teaspoon salt
1¼ envelopes yeast

1 cup warm water
2 cups Plain Tomato Sauce
(page 34)

Mix all ingredients together. Knead until smooth. Place in large bowl, cover, and let rise in a warm place until double in size. Divide into 2 pieces. Stretch and fit each piece on greased 12-inch pizza pan or pie plate. Top with tomato sauce and bake in 400°F oven 20 to 25 minutes.
Makes 2 pies.

VARIATIONS
The following is a list of ingredients for topping pizza after the tomato sauce has been spread on the dough; of course, the only important one is your imagination! These ingredients may be sprinkled on at random, or, if you're feeling particularly creative, you can arrange them in intricate patterns.

Anchovies
Black olives, sliced
Capers
Cheese, grated
Eggplant, diced and cooked
Green olives, sliced
Green pepper, chopped
Ground beef and pork,
  mixed

Mozzarella, sliced
Mushrooms, sliced
Onions, sliced or chopped
Pepperoni sausage, sliced
Sardines
Sausage, sliced
Tuna fish

COLD POTATOES
Patate Fredde

2 cups cold, boiled potatoes,
  diced
3 tablespoons olive oil
1 tablespoon red wine vinegar

2 tablespoons green onion,
  chopped
Salt and pepper to taste

Mix all ingredients, chill, and serve.
Serves 2 to 4.

Gioia Del Studente

1 tablespoon olive oil	*Salt and pepper to taste*
1 clove garlic, sliced thin	*1 slice fresh Italian bread*

Sprinkle first 3 ingredients over slice of bread and eat immediately!
Makes 1 serving.

GLOSSARY

When we were first married, my husband devised an ingenious phonetic spelling for some of the most common Italian foods. I'm passing it on to you because I think that it's always helpful to be able to pronounce what you've cooked.

Some of the words look very strange when spelled this way. But don't underestimate them because they look funny — they work.

Acciughe	A-cheej	Anchovies
Aceto	A-che-toe	Vinegar
Affogato	Ah-foo-cot	Smothered
Aglio	A-lio	Garlic
Agnello	Ah-ny-low	Lamb
Albicocca	Ahl-bee-co-ca	Apricot
Alla	Ah-la	In the style of
Amaretti	Ama-rre-tee	Macaroons
Anitra	Ah-nee-tra	Duck
Antipasto	Onti-pastoe	Appetizer
Aragosta	Ah-rra-ghost-ah	Lobster
Arancia	Ah-rahn-chee-ah	Orange
Arrostito	Ah-rrow-stee-toe	Roast
Asparagi	Ah-spa-rr-gee	Asparagus
Baccalà	Bah-ka-la	Dried codfish
Basilico	Bosh-a-lee-go	Basil
Bianco	Bee-on-co	White
Biscotti	Bee-scow-tee	Biscuits
Bistecca	Bee-stek-ka	Beefsteak
Bollito	Bow-lee-toe	Boiled
Braciola	Bra-shawl	Rolled steak
Braciuolini	Bra-shawl-lee-nee	Little, rolled steak
Brodo	Brough-dough	Broth
Buccia	Boo-cha	Rind
Budino	Boo-dee-no	Pudding

Cacciatora	Kah-cha-torry	Hunter's style
Caffè	Ka-fay	Coffee
Calamai	Kala-mod	Squid
Caldo	Kal-dough	Hot
Cannella	Ka-nell-la	Cinnamon
Cannelloni	Con-a-low-nee	Little pasta pipes
Capellini	Cop-a-leeny	Very thin spaghetti
Capitone	Cop-pee-tone	Eels
Capocollo	Cop-a-gaul	Italian smoked pork
Cappelletti	Cop-pa-letty	Little hats (pasta)
Capperi	Ka-parry	Capers
Carciofi	Car-chio-fee	Artichokes
Carne	Karn-ay	Meat
Carote	Ka-rroe-tee	Carrots
Castagne	Kast-tannia	Chestnuts
Cavolfiore	Kavow-ll-fee-ow-rree	Cauliflower
Cavolo	Ka-vo-low	Cabbage
Ceci	Chee-chee	Chick peas
Cervo	Cher-vo	Venison
Cicoria	Chee-co-ria	Chicory
Cicoria fina	Chee-co-ria fee-na	Dandelion
Ciliegia	Chee-lee-gia	Cherry
Cioccolata	Chio-co-lottow	Chocolate
Cipolla	Chi-polla	Onion
Con	Con	With
Coniglio	Con-neel	Rabbit
Coscia	Coe-shah	Leg
Costoletta	Kost-teh-letty	Chop
Cotoletta	Coa-tow-letta	Cutlet
Cotto	Kow-toe	Cooked
Crema	Kreem-ma	Cream
Crosta	Crost-ta	Crust
Crudo	Croo-dough	Raw
Cuore	Co-rr-ee	Heart
Ditalini	Deet-ta-leen-nee	Tiny, round, hollow noodles
Dolce	Dole-shay	Sweet

E	Aye	And
Erbe	Air-bee	Herbs
Escarola	Shka-dole	Escarole
Fagiano	Fhaj-ee-ah-no	Pheasant
Fagioli	Fa-jole-ee	Beans
Fagiolini	Fa-jio-leen-nee	String beans
Fegatini	Feh-ga-tee-nee	Chicken livers
Fegato	Feh-ga-toe	Liver
Fettuccine	Fet-too-chee-nee	Wide noodles
Finocchio	Fee-no-kio	Italian celery
Formaggio	For-moj	Cheese
Forno	For-no	Oven
Fresca	Fresh-ka	Fresh
Fritto	Free-toe	Fried
Frutta	Froo-ta	Fruit
Funghi	Foonj	Mushrooms
Gamberetti	Gom-ber-ret-ti	Shrimp
Gamberi	Gom-be-rry	Crawfish
Gnocchi	Nnio-key	Dumplings
Griglia	Grree-lia	Grill
Imbottito	Imm-bow-tee-toe	Stuffed
Insalata	Inn-zol-lod	Salad
Lasagne	Lah-zan-ya	Broad, flat noodles
Latte	Lotty	Milk
Lenticchie	Len-teek	Lentils
Limone	Lee-moan	Lemon
Linguini	Lin-gween-nee	Flat, narrow noodles
Lombata	Lom-bow	Loin
Maiale	My-ee-lay	Pork
Mandorla	Mon-dow-r-la	Almond
Manicotti	Mon-a-gaut	Rolled, stuffed noodles
Manzo	Mon-zow	Beef

Marinara	Mah-ree-nah-rha	Mariner style
Maruzelle	Ma-rroo-tz	Large pasta seashells
Medualla	Me-doo-la	Brain
Melanzana	Melon-zon	Eggplant
Melone	Mel-lone	Melon
Merluzzo	Mare-lootz-zow	Whiting
Minestrone	Min-a-strown	Vegetable soup
Mista	Mes-sta	Mixed
Mozzarella	Moot-sa-dell	Mild, white cheese
Olio	Oh-lio	Oil
Oregano	Ow-rheg-ah-no	Oregano herb
Panato	Pahn-not-toe	Breaded
Pane	Pahn	Bread
Panino	Pa-nee-no	Roll
Panino imbottito	Pa-nee-no imm-bow-tee-toe	Sandwich
Parmesan	Par-mee-john	Cheese for grating
Pasta	Pahst-ta	Dough, macaroni
Pasticcino	Pahst-ee-chee-no	Cookie, cake
Pasticcio	Pahst-ee-cho	Pie
Pastina	Pah-steen-ah	Tiny, flake pasta
Patata	Pa-ta-tay	Potato
Pecorino	Pay-kow-ree-no	Goat's milk cheese, for grating
Peperoni	Pepper-own-nee	Green peppers
Pesca	Paish-a	Peach
Pesce	Paish	Fish
Petto	Pet-toe	Breast
Piccione	Peek-ee-own	Pigeon
Piselli	Pi-sell-ly	Peas
Pizza	Peet-za	Type of pie
Pollo	Pow-lo	Chicken, fowl
Polpette	Poll-petty	Meatballs
Polpettone	Poll-pet-tone-nay	Meat loaf
Pomodoro	Po-mo-dough-row	Tomato

Prosciutto	Pro-shoot	Italian ham
Provolone	Pro-vo-lone	Mild, yellow cheese
Ravioli	Rah-vio-lee	Stuffed pasta pillows
Ricotta	Ree-kaught	Italian cottage cheese
Ripieno	Ree-pee-no	Full, stuffed, stuffing
Riso	Rree-sow	Rice
Salmone	Sal-mown-neh	Salmon
Salsa	Sol-sa	Sauce
Salsiccia	Saw-zeech	Sausage
Salsiccia con peperoni	Saw-zeech con pepper-own-nee	Dry, smoked sausage with peppers
Scasciatta	Scoch-yatd	Smashed, pounded
Sedano	See-donny	Celery
Spiedi	Speed-dee	Spits or skewers
Spinaci	Spee-nah-kee	Spinach
Spumoni	Spoo-mow-nee	Italian ice cream
Spuntino	Spoon-teen-ow	Snack
Stufato	Stoo-fa-tow	Stew
Timballo	Teem-boll-low	Pie
Tonno	Tow-no	Tuna fish
Torrone	Tow-rrow-nee	Nougat candy
Trippa	Tree-pa	Tripe
Trota	Trow-ta	Trout
Tufoli	Too-fow-lee	Hollow pasta for stuffing
Umido	Oo-mee-dough	Stew
Uovo	Oo-vo	Egg
Verde	Vair-dee	Green
Vino	Vee-no	Wine

Vitello	Vee-tell-low	Veal
Vongole	Von-go-lay	Mussels or Clams
Zabaglione	Zob-a-lee-yo-nee	Wine custard
Zucchero	Zoo-kair-row	Sugar
Zucchini	Zoo-kee-nee	Italian squash
Zuppa	Zoo-pa	Soup

Now you can go into the Italian store equipped with the proper information and the correct pronunciations. But how many beans do you want? Which ones? And how much are they? I hope the following list of numbers and phrases will be of help to you. Of course, you must remember the most important thing of all — speak up *loud and clear* or you'll never be heard!

Good Luck! Ciao!

1	Uno	Oon-o
2	Due	Dewey
3	Tre	Tray
4	Quattro	Quat-trow
5	Cinque	Ching-quay
6	Sei	Say-ee
7	Sette	Set-tay
8	Otto	Aught-toe
9	Nove	No-vay
10	Dieci	Dee-ay-chee

Hello	Buon giorno	Bwohn jor-noe
How are you?	Come Sta?	Coma-stah
Please	Per piacere	Pear pee-a-cher-eh
Pound	Libbra	Lee-bra
Sliced thin	Tagliatti fini	Tag-lee-ah-tee fee-nee
This one	Questa	Quest-ah
Them	Quelli	Quell-ee
Those	Quelli là	Quell-ee-la
Half	Mezzo	Met-zo
Dozen	Dozzina	Doe-zeen-ah
Chopped	Tagliatti in pezzi	Tag-lee-ah-tee in pet-ze
Little bit	Un poco	Oon poc-co
Some more	Di piu	Dee-pew
That's enough	Abasta	Ah-bahst-ah
How much?	Quanto?	Quan-toe
Thank you	Grazie	Gratz-zee
Goodbye	Ciao	Chow

INDEX